Interview Styles & Strategies

Professional Development Series

Author:

Aggie White, M.A.
Central Carolina Technical College
Sumter, South Carolina

SOUTH-WESTERN
™
THOMSON LEARNING

Australia • Canada • Mexico • Singapore • Spain • United Kingdom • United States

SOUTH-WESTERN
™
THOMSON LEARNING

Interview Styles & Strategies
By Aggie White

Vice President/Editor-in-Chief
Jack Calhoun

Vice President/Executive Publisher:
Dave Shaut

Team Leader:
Karen Schmohe

Project Manager:
Dr. Inell Bolls

Production Editor:
Carol Spencer

Production Manager:
Tricia Boies

Executive Marketing Manager:
Carol Volz

Marketing Manager:
Chris McNamee

Marketing Coordinator:
Cira Brown

Manufacturing Manager:
Charlene Taylor

Design Project Manager:
Stacy Jenkins Shirley

Cover and Internal Design:
Grannan Graphic Design, Ltd.

Copy Editor:
Marianne Miller

Compositor:
Electro-Publishing

Printer:
Edwards Bros./Ann Arbor

Rights and Permissions Manager:
Linda Ellis

For more information, contact South-Western
5191 Natorp Boulevard
Mason, OH 45040
Or, visit our Internet site at
www.swlearning.com.

For permission to use material from t
text or product, contact us by
Phone: 1-800-730-2214,
Fax: 1-800-730-2215, or
www.thomsonrights.com.

Gain the Insight to Professional Success

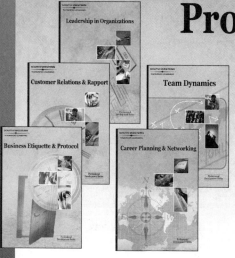

Keeping pace with today's competitive marketplace is a challenge.

Although technology has enabled us to communicate and produce in ways we never thought possible, there are other essential elements to achieving professional success. *The Professional Development Series* is a quick and practical resource for learning non-technical strategies and tactics.

0-538-72463-3	Business Etiquette & Protocol
0-538-72527-3	Customer Relations & Rapport
0-538-72484-6	Leadership in Organizations
0-538-72474-9	Career Planning & Networking
0-538-72485-4	Team Dynamics

The 10-Hour Series

This series enables you to become proficient in a variety of technical skills in only a short amount of time through ten quick and easy lessons.

0-538-69458-0	E-mail in 10 Hours
0-538-68928-5	Composing at the Computer
0-538-69849-7	Electronic Business Presentations

Quick Skills Series

Quickly sharpen the interpersonal skills you need for job success and professional development with the Quick Skills Series. This series features career-related scenarios for relevant and real application of skills.

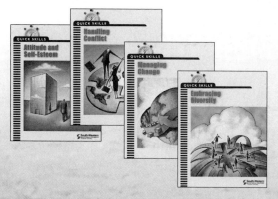

0-538-69026-7	Attitude and Self Esteem
0-538-69833-0	Handling Conflict
0-538-69839-X	Managing Change
0-538-69842-X	Embracing Diversity

SOUTH-WESTERN
™
THOMSON LEARNING

Join us on the Internet
www.swep.com

Contents

Preface

The interview is the most critical stage in the job-seeking process. Most employers make a hiring decision based on the applicant's performance during the interview. In today's world of business, finding the right job requires an investment of time, energy, and resources on the part of the job seeker. The field can be very competitive; and in many cases, the most qualified applicant does not get the job. The applicant who does get the job offer is well prepared with effective interviewing skills and techniques. In addition, individuals interview more often today because having one job for life is a thing of the past. Technology has had an impact on how and where interviews take place, and there are certain techniques applicants can use to give them an edge. The one-on-one interview is still one of the most popular styles. However, new formats are being used as the workplace becomes team-oriented and more people in the organization are provided the opportunity to have input into the hiring process. *Interview Styles and Strategies* provides strategies and guidelines for users to follow during the job search.

Message to the User

Interview Styles and Strategies is designed to assist the person who is interviewing or planning to interview for a job. The module provides a guide to understanding the interviewing process and what the job seeker's responsibilities are at each stage in the process. The module provides helpful hints and tips on choosing the appropriate attire for the interview and tips on appropriate behavior and etiquette. In addition, it offers 25 frequently asked interview questions with suggestions on how to develop effective answers to these questions. Upon completion of this module, a job seeker should be prepared to face the interview with confidence and to perform effectively.

Features

Each topic begins with clear goals entitled "At the Core." A list of key concepts learned is presented at the end of each topic.

A pre- and post-assessment activity is also included at the beginning and end of the module that may be used as a fun, nongraded activity. *Interview Styles and Strategies* is organized into eight topics that cover what the interview is and is not, most frequently asked questions, styles and types of interviews, strategies for planning and practicing, strategies for interviewing effectively, strategies for handling the tough questions, strategies for evaluating performance, and strategies for negotiating the deal. Online resources for further research are provided for every topic. The three culminating activities at the end of Topic 8 may be used as a final assessment tool upon completion of this module.

About the Author

Aggie White is an educator by profession. She graduated from The Ohio State University with a bachelor of science degree and taught in the field of education as an elementary school teacher; she also worked several years in business. Upon receiving a masters degree from the University of South Carolina, she transferred to post-secondary education. She has served as an instructor and a department chair in the Office Systems Technology Department of Central Carolina Technical College for the last ten years. She currently serves as registrar for the college, but continues to teach on a part-time basis.

Pre-Assessment Activity

TRUE/FALSE

Directions: Read each of the following statements carefully. Circle T if the statement is true and F if the statement is false.

1. T F A job interview is an opportunity for an employer to examine the qualifications of a job seeker for a position in the company.

2. T F At the beginning of the interview, the interviewer will often converse with you on general topics, such as the weather or local interest issues. Do not be concerned about your responses, as these discussions have nothing to do with the job interview.

3. T F Technology has had minimal impact on interviewing techniques.

4. T F A poor first impression can be overcome.

5. T F Being prepared to handle frequently asked questions is the best way to help you relax and relieve some of the stress and nervousness associated with interviewing.

6. T F During an informal/discussion interview, the interviewer usually asks the same questions of each job applicant for a position.

7. T F The purpose of the meal interview is to observe how an applicant conducts himself or herself in a social situation.

8. T F The most qualified applicant always gets the job.

9. T F A personal mission statement should define who you are, why you exist, and what you will do to become the person you want to be.

10. T F Corporate culture is the environment of unwritten rules of behavior and values that influence the way business is conducted in the workplace.

11. T F Nervousness occurs before and during the interview because of the fear of rejection.

12. T F A calming technique used to control nervousness is concentrating on the outcome of the interview.

13. T F "What foreign languages do you speak?" is a legal question.

14. T F "Are you a Democrat or a Republican?" is a legal question.

15. T F If you are not interested in the position for which you interviewed, you do not need to send a follow-up thank you letter to the interviewer.

MULTIPLE CHOICE

Directions: Read each of the following statements carefully. Circle the letter of the best response for each statement:

1. Your goal as the job seeker is to
   a. understand what the employer wants and try to match your skills and abilities to those needs.
   b. use the interview as an opportunity to learn more about the position and the organization.
   c. make an effective and professional impression on the interviewer(s).
   d. all of the above.

2. If an interviewer requests that you "Tell me about yourself," your best response would include
   a. a detailed discussion of your work experience.
   b. an overview of the work and education, that have prepared you for the position.
   c. a description of your plans for child care.
   d. personal information that may help the employer make an informed decision.

3. Your reference list should NOT include the names and addresses of the following people:
   a. friends who can attest to your loyalty and dependability
   b. supervisors or instructors who can attest to the quality and quantity of your work
   c. relatives who can attest to your honesty and reliability
   d. coworkers who can attest to your teamwork skills and work ethic

4. Questions about salary expectations should be
   a. answered by requesting information about the company's benefit package.
   b. answered with a specific amount that you learned from your research.
   c. avoided and left up to the generosity of the employer.
   d. deflected and a vague, nonspecific answer given.

5. Which of the following interview types deliberately set up uncomfortable situations for the applicant?
   a. selection
   b. hiring
   c. screening
   d. stress

6. The most common deficiency among job applicants is the lack of
   a. knowledge about the company with whom they are interviewing.
   b. preparation to discuss career plans and goals.
   c. enthusiasm and interest in the company or the position.
   d. experience and preparation for the position.

7. The documentation you need to gather before interviewing includes
   a. your resume.
   b. a list of questions to ask.
   c. your social security card.
   d. all of the above.

8. A self-confident person
   a. does not possess positive self-esteem.
   b. does not have a positive sense of self-worth.
   c. is not self-centered.
   d. all of the above.

9. During your question time, which of the following questions should you NOT ask?
   a. What benefits do you offer?
   b. Why is the position available?
   c. What qualities are you seeking in the candidate for the position?
   d. When are you anticipating making a decision about the position?

10. Which of the following is a good strategy to use to overcome nervousness?
    a. Eat a good breakfast.
    b. Think of the interview as an information-gathering process.
    c. Concentrate on the importance of the interview in meeting your goals.
    d. Focus on the importance of your performance in the outcome of the interview.

11. Which of the following is the best strategy to use when answering an illegal interview question?
    a. Answer the question.
    b. Deflect the question.
    c. Deal with the concern behind the question, and ignore the question itself.
    d. Refuse to answer the question.

12. After the interview, the most important thing to do is
    a. evaluate your performance.
    b. get clothing ready for the next interview.
    c. thank your references.
    d. wait patiently for the employer to call.

13. In your thank-you letter to the interviewer for a position you want, you should
    a. express your appreciation for his or her time and consideration of your skills and abilities.
    b. restate your interest in the position.
    c. explain why you want to work for the company.
    d. all of the above.

14. When the job offer is made, you should
    a. accept the offer if you want the job.
    b. request thinking time.
    c. research salaries in comparable industries.
    d. compare the offer to what your friends are earning.

15. A factor to consider when facing the salary issue includes
    a. geographical location.
    b. your qualifications.
    c. the value of the benefits package offered.
    d. all of the above.

1
The Interview: What It Is and Is Not

AT THE CORE
This topic examines:

➤ **THE PURPOSE OF THE INTERVIEW**
➤ **THE INTERVIEW PROCESS**
➤ **THE IMPACT OF TECHNOLOGY ON INTERVIEWS**
➤ **TYPICAL INTERVIEW MYTHS**
➤ **TRUTHS ABOUT INTERVIEWS**

> *Strategy #1: Concentrate on one thing—the invitation to an interview.*

An interview is an opportunity for an employer to examine, usually in a question-and-answer exchange, the qualifications of a job seeker for a position in the company. Although not always considered, an interview is also an opportunity for the job seeker to examine the company and the position to see if they are appealing. Notice the use of the word *opportunity*. Both parties should take advantage of the opportunity to learn as much as possible about each other. In most cases for the employer, the interview is one of the major determining factors to hire or not to hire. If the employer believes the job seeker fits the needs of the company, an offer will be made. In many cases, the interviewee does not take advantage of the opportunity to determine if the company is a good fit. The interviewee is just interested in getting the job.

The Purpose of the Interview

The job interview is an exchange between two entities: the employer and the applicant or job seeker. This exchange usually takes the format of a question-answer session(s) where the employer asks the questions and the applicant answers the questions. From the impression the applicant makes and the answers he or she provides to the questions, the employer will make a decision.

©PhotoDisc, Inc.

From the employer's perspective, he or she is looking for an employee who will fit the needs of the company. The employer will be searching for a candidate with the skills, personality, experience, and potential to meet the requirements established or perceived to be required by the organization. Therefore, before interviewing applicants for a position, the employer must clearly establish what skills, abilities, talents, experience, and personality the company needs to fill the position. The employer should keep these requirements in mind throughout the interview process.

From your point of view as a job seeker, you must understand what the employer wants and try to match your skills and abilities to those needs. Your first goal is to research and learn about the company, its product, its culture, and the job description of the position for which you are being interviewed. You want to learn as much as you can to prepare yourself for what the employer wants.

Your second goal is to use the interview as an opportunity to learn more about the position and the organization. Be prepared to ask questions. Try to get answers to the questions you could not get from your research. For example, by asking how you will be evaluated, you discover the supervisor's expectations. Just as it is important for the employer to learn if you will meet the needs of the company, it is equally important for you to determine if the company is going to meet your needs as an employee.

Therefore, the interview is a two-way exchange of impressions and information. The employer will make a decision based on a first impression and your body language, tone of voice, and facial expressions, as well as information you express directly or imply. If the overall impression the employer receives is positive and he or she believes you meet the needs of the company, something very negative would have to come up to change the employer's mind when he or she reviews your resume and application and checks your references. If the first impression is negative, it is very likely the employer will not bother to review your resume or check references.

As an applicant, you, too, should make a judgment based on the same elements of the exchange. The impressions and information you receive will assist you in making a decision. Before making a final decision, however, you should review your research about the company and speak again with people you contacted during your research about the company. Determine if this is the environment in which you want to work.

From both the employer's and the applicant's perspective, the interview should be an investigation into each other. A student had just completed her associate degree in Office Systems Technology, so she placed her resume with an employment company. An employer was searching for an employee to fill an open position in his company. He spotted this student's resume and said, "I'll take this one." She was hired on the spot—no interview. She accepted the position. On her first day of work, she learned she would be driving a fork lift and wearing a hard hat and that most of the job duties did not match her skills and talents. Understandably, she resigned before she even started the job.

Several things happened here. The employer selected an employee based only on the resume and obviously had not determined the needs of his organization. The employment agency did not carefully screen the applicants and attempt to match them to the needs of the employer. The job seeker just wanted a job and did not inquire or request an interview to learn about the position. Unfortunately, everyone involved lost time, energy, and money. An interview could have quickly shown both parties the unsuitability of the applicant for the position.

As the single most important element in getting a job, think of the interview as an opportunity to sell your skills and abilities. Match your talents to the needs of the company. Listen carefully to determine if the company can meet your needs as an employee.

The Interview Process

Generally, all interviews follow a similar pattern. By being aware of the pattern, you relieve some of the anxiety and stress associated with the interview process. Although there may be some deviation from the routine, all interviews generally begin with a meeting and greeting time, proceed to a question-and-answer session, and end with a summary/conclusion period.

Stage one is the meeting and greeting process. Names are exchanged and introductions are made. Conversation is usually general, and innocuous topics such as the weather, local events, and travel to the interview are discussed. These discussions all serve as icebreakers. The interviewer may attempt to establish rapport or place the interviewee at ease and provide a more comfortable environment. During this stage, you want to remember names and titles and try to relax for the questions to come.

> **TIP** Use the interviewer's name. Using the name delivers a message of respect and recognition.

Stage two is the question-and-answer period during which questions are asked by the interviewer and answered by you. Your skills, abilities, experience, and interpersonal relationships are typical topics for this stage. While you are selling yourself and your abilities, the interviewer is sizing you up for compatibility or a fit with the company and the position.

> **TIP** Relate your qualifications and experiences fully. If you have never worked full-time, speak about your volunteer, extracurricular, and part-time work experience.

Stage three provides an opportunity for you to ask any questions you may have about the company or the position. Be prepared to take advantage of the chance. Prepare a list of questions ahead of time. Include any questions that were generated by the interview. Your purpose during this stage is to get as much information as possible.

During the final stage, the interviewer begins to summarize and conclude the interview. Your objective at this stage is to learn the timeline for the hiring process, establish how you will be notified, and receive permission to call for progress updates. Be sure to thank the interviewer for his or her time and consideration, then leave.

Impact of Technology on Interviews

Technology has made everyone virtually next-door neighbors. Businesses are finding that the search for employees can be global rather than local. The World Wide Web has changed how job seekers learn of job openings and how employers find potential employees. Company web sites now post available positions. Numerous web sites post resumes of job seekers, allowing employers to search for applicants with the desired skills; and vice versa, a job seeker can search for job openings. Technology is also impacting the interview.

The Telephone. The telephone interview may seem to be the least difficult and least stressful type of interview, but in reality it is the most difficult. Telephone interviews are used most often as a screening tool to avoid the expense of travel for a prospective candidate who lives some distance from the interview location. Because there are no visual clues, both parties must use effective oral communication techniques to send the right message. Vocal tone, word usage, and enunciation are critical elements. Speak directly into the telephone. Try to give more than one-word answers to explain your talents and abilities. For example, if an interviewer asks if you have experience with Microsoft® Word. Rather than answering "yes," explain that you took a college course on Word, earned an A, and successfully completed the MOUS Certification Test at the proficient level. Take notes during the interview. They will become valuable when you have a face-to-face meeting.[1]

When the telephone is used as an interviewing medium, those involved must remember that articulation, tone of voice, and choice of words are important due to the lack of visual cues and body language.

©PhotoDisc, Inc.

To give yourself an edge with a telephone interview, dress professionally for it. You will project a more professional image if you dress for the part, rather than slouching around in pajamas or sweats. Try to convey a positive attitude by projecting enthusiasm and an upbeat attitude. Have your resume and other notes ready. Try to avoid shuffling papers, as it may send crackling noises over the phone lines. Eliminate all possible distractions and interruptions by enabling call waiting or another electronic interrupter. Request family members to leave the house, or find a room that is quiet and isolated.

TIP During the telephone interview, stand up and speak. You will have more oxygen flowing if you stand and breathe deeply.

How important is the telephone in the job-hunting process? The telephone will become your primary source of contact with potential employers. It will be a primary resource in gaining necessary information. The first contact an employer or a representative of the employer may have with you is a telephone call. This may come after he or she receives your letter of application and resume.

How you answer the phone and how you address the caller will establish a first impression. Make it a good one. If you have an answering machine, be sure your recorded message sounds professional. Many people eliminate themselves from further consideration for a position because the message on their answering machine creates a less than professional image. Using a less than professional message, may leave the caller with a question about your use of good judgment.

Although the telephone is used by business as an important screening interview tool, it is rarely the choice of media for the final interview. On some occasions, an applicant may be interviewed from a distance via the telephone so both parties can determine if travel and a face-to-face meeting would be profitable.

Videoconferencing. Videoconferencing is a system of transmitting audio and video signals between individuals at distant locations. Individuals can see and hear each other. The videoconference is an option if distance and travel expenses are prohibitive factors. Be aware of two minor problems you may experience using teleconferencing equipment. First, the conference is held in real time but there may be a few seconds' delay of the audio behind the video. This takes a bit of adjustment by both parties. It may take a few attempts to avoid talking over each other. Secondly, what you wear is critically important. Avoid red (men, particularly with ties) and any bright, vibrant color. Also avoid anything that has a pattern. The transmission of the color and patterns can appear distorted and rainbow, which becomes very distracting. Even with these two potential difficulties, videoconferencing is an effective tool to use when distance is a problem.

Some companies have access to video conferencing equipment and can set up an interview time with another branch of the company or with a service provider. This eliminates the lack of visual cues that occurs with using the telephone. Therefore, it is more effective than the telephone. One of the largest obstacles to videoconferencing in the past was the amount of bandwidth needed and the picture quality. However, the technology is steadily improving.

Computer-to-Computer. Within the last several years, new software packages have become available that provide video transmittal from one computer to another. NetMeeting™ is one of these software packages. Participants can arrange an interview anytime and anywhere, providing a savings in travel time and expense, meals, and accommodations. Computer-to-computer interviewing is becoming more common. It is not as effective as face-to-face interviewing, but it certainly eliminates the problems associated with telephone interviews. The software package NetMeeting can turn a personal computer into effective videoconferencing equipment.

I recently had a unique experience using this software. I was assisting an instructor in a class project by interviewing all of her students. She and I created a job description, and students sent me their letters of application and resumes. We set up an appointment for each student. Because the class was online, we had one student who was living in Italy. We used NetMeeting to conduct that interview.

The student and I both needed a PC and the software, Internet access, a camera, and a microphone. Taking into consideration the time difference, we arranged a convenient time that met both our needs. We connected using the software. It was just like the videoconference described previously. There was a time delay between video and voice, but we quickly adjusted. She gave a very good interview, and overall it proved to be an effective method of interviewing a truly distant potential employee. Computers are sure to become a common medium for communicating and interviewing.

Typical Interview Myths

Misinformation about interviews is common and only adds to the stress and anxiety they can produce. Let's look at some of these myths and get the real story.

1. **My resume will get me the job.** Wrong. Your resume is designed to get you the interview; interviews get you the job. The only time the resume may have gotten an applicant a job was in the situation described earlier, which turned out to be a disaster for all parties involved. Your resume should look professional and clearly outline your skills and experiences. Your resume should entice the interviewer to arrange an interview. You also need the opportunity the interview presents to determine if you want the position with the company.

2. **First impressions cannot be overcome.** Wrong. First impressions are critical and difficult to overcome, but they are not impossible to change. It takes extraordinary effort and strong interviewing skills to erase a poor first impression. Effective preparation should eliminate the chance of making a poor first impression, but if for some reason you sense a negative reaction, hone your listening skills, focus on strong and confident answers, and ask effective questions. Take heart; you can recover.

3. **A poorly answered question is a disaster, and there is no recovery.** Wrong. You have another opportunity. You can contemplate a more effective answer and submit that answer in your thank-you letter. Simply state in the letter that when assessing your performance and responses, you concluded that the questions concerning…required a more extensive answer. Then proceed to give a more effective response.

4. **All interviewers know how to interview effectively.** Wrong. Most interviewers do not know how to use the time provided to get the answers they really need. In fact, most interviewers do not know

the questions to ask to obtain the information they need to make an informed decision. Some interviewers do not know what is legal to ask. Some interviewers do not know how to prepare effectively for the interview. Therefore, you may be in the driver's seat by providing them with the information you want them to know.

5. **The most qualified person gets the job.** Wrong. Often the most qualified person does not get the job. There are many factors that enter into the decision to hire. Skills, abilities, experience, and education are just some of the factors. Probably the most important reason you are hired is because the interviewer likes you. The interviewer likes your skills, talents, experience, and education; but he or she also likes your looks, your personality, your presentation, and so on. Interviewers will rarely recommend for hire someone they do not like. Therefore, your goal is to make the interviewer like you.[2]

Truths About Interviews

In addition to the myths and misconceptions about interviews that abound, there are some basic truths of which all interviewees should be aware. Knowing these basic truths will assist you in avoiding the simple faux pas.

1. **Most interview appointments are made by telephone.** When the employer receives your resume and moves you into the "potential" column, a date for an interview is established. Today employers usually forgo writing a letter, using the telephone to call the potential employee instead. Therefore, you should be prepared for the initial call to plan the interview date. Have a professional message on your answering machine. Have a calendar and pen or pencil beside the phone so you are prepared when the phone call comes.

2. **The first five minutes are the most important time in the interview.** This is the time when the interviewer makes the initial impression that will sit firmly in his or her mind. You will have answered a question or two, so the interviewer will get a more solid impression. (The factors included in making that impression are how you look, stand, sit, vocalize, and express yourself.) The first

impression sets the tone for the remainder of the interview and may determine its outcome.

3. **Interviewers can be nervous too.** Do not be fooled into thinking that you are the only one in the room who is nervous. For example, in a panel interview, interviewers may be performing in front of their contemporaries or supervisors; as a result, they may feel some pressure. In addition, hiring decisions are extremely important to a company because mistakes can be very costly.

4. **Networking, recommendations from insiders, and knowledge of your abilities and work ethic are more likely to get you the interview than your resume and letter of application.** If a company can get inside information about you and your abilities, you are far more likely to get an interview than a person who just submits a resume and a letter of application. Therefore, use your network to assist you. You also have a better chance of getting a job offer if your interviewers have received positive input about you.

5. **Preparation is the most important strategy as you ready yourself for the interview.** Preparation is the secret. Preparation should be done in every step of the process. You can prepare for 80 percent of the questions the interviewer is likely to ask you. These are great odds in the game of interviewing. It is up to you.[3]

RECAP OF KEY CONCEPTS

- An interview is a two-way exchange between an employer and an applicant to gather as much information about each other so an effective hiring decision can be made.

- The typical interview is face-to-face and one-on-one and follows a specific pattern. Interviews usually begin with the interviewer and interviewee taking time to build rapport. Next comes the question-and-answer period. Then the interview progresses to the summary and conclusion.

- Technology is impacting the way interviews are conducted. This technology includes the telephone, videoconferencing, and computer-to-computer.

- There are many myths about the interview: My resume will get me the job; first impressions cannot be overcome; a poorly answered question is a disaster, and there is no recovery; all interviewers know how to interview effectively; and the most qualified person gets the job.

- In addition to the myths about interviews that abound, there are some basic truths: Interview appointments are usually made by telephone, the first five minutes are critical, and interviewers can be nervous too. Your network is very important and can give you a leading edge. Preparation is the secret to success.

2
Frequently Asked Questions

AT THE CORE
This topic examines:

➤ TWENTY-FIVE FREQUENTLY ASKED INTERVIEW QUESTIONS
➤ A COMPREHENSIVE LIST OF FREQUENTLY ASKED QUESTIONS

> *Strategy #2: You are the most qualified person to talk about you, so make it good.*

Interview questions vary in number and type dependent upon the job for which you are applying and the style of the interview being held. In other words, the questions for a screening interview are asked to determine your minimum qualifications for a position and vary substantially from the questions of a hiring interview to determine if you are the best candidate for a position. However, some questions are frequently asked in all interviews.

The following FAQs are not in any special order, and some variations of the questions may be asked. Being prepared to handle these FAQs not only boost your confidence level but also help you relax and relieve some of the stress and nervousness associated with the interviewing process. Some of the questions are direct yes, no, or one-word answers; others require some thought and extended explanations or descriptions. Although strategies will be discussed to answer these questions effectively, always remember that honesty is the only policy in the job-seeking process.

Twenty-five Frequently Asked Interview Questions

- **Personal Interest and Character**

Tell me about yourself. Answer with a focus on your preparation for the position for which you are applying. Discuss your educational preparation and work experience that would directly impact your effectiveness as an employee. Keep your answer concise and focused. Do not ramble, providing every detail of your experiences. Do not give personal information such as age, marital status, or number of children. Do not start the answer with "My name is. . ."; the interviewer already knows your name.

What personal skill or habit have you struggled to improve? Describe a skill/habit you have improved. Explain how you have improved the skill or eliminated the bad habit. By the end of your answer, your interviewer/employer must believe this skill has solidly improved or the habit no longer exists.

When you are not at work, do you prefer a planned schedule for activities or are you spontaneous in whatever happens? Be cautious when you answer this question. Consider carefully the position for which you are applying. A salesperson would not perform well in an environment that was structured and planned. He or she must be flexible and able to handle a change of plans or strategies quickly. Therefore, someone who plans and schedules weekend activities probably would not function well as a salesperson. In the reverse, a civil engineer's position is rigid and structured. Therefore, planning and scheduling of weekend time would be acceptable for a person interviewing for a job as an engineer.

What do you do in your spare time? Most companies are looking for well-rounded individuals or people who have interests other than work. The interviewer is interested in whether your play is compatible with your work. Perhaps you enjoy sports. An employer knows sports and exercise help reduce stress and increase the possibility of good health. Coaching or teaching sports is considered community involvement. All of these are considered positives in the interviewer's mind. Whether you are a volunteer with youth or the elderly, an avid reader, or a lover of the great outdoors, provide information that would cause the interviewer to form a positive impression.

©PhotoDisc, Inc.

What is your favorite book, movie, or play? What did you learn as a result of reading or seeing this book, movie, or play? Again, the interviewer is looking for a person with interests outside of work. Are those interests compatible with work? Select a movie, book, or play you particularly liked. Then be able to discuss what you learned from it and how you have applied what you learned.

- **Skill Preparation and Qualifications**

Describe your greatest strength and greatest weakness. Discussing your greatest strength is an opportunity to sell yourself and those qualities the employer needs. Is your greatest strength your skills and knowledge, your ability to get along with people, or your effective customer service techniques? Everyone has strengths. Assess yours; then select the ones that best suit the needs of the employer.

When responding to the weakness portion of the question, you have several choices. Everyone has areas for improvement. Assess the areas in your work that you could improve. For example, perhaps your knowledge of Excel® or Access® could be stronger. Explain that you are not as knowledgeable as you would like to be, but your plan is to master the program and take the MOUS Certification Test within six months. You want to convey to the interviewer that you are aware of your weakness and that you have a plan or a goal set to improve or eliminate the deficiency.

Another option is to select a characteristic that a person would normally consider a weakness but an employer would consider positive. It should be job-related. Suppose the position for which you are applying is a customer service representative and you are a very caring person. You might say, "Sometimes I get too involved with people and their problems." Normally a person would find the shouldering of others' problems a negative, but an employer who is looking for a person who will go the extra mile for a customer would find this to be an asset.

Why should we hire you? This is your opportunity to sell yourself. Do not hesitate to discuss your strengths: your skills, talents, and abilities. Focus on those strengths that are desirable and needed by the company.

Describe your educational background. The interviewer is primarily interested in formal education (high school, college, or vocational) that has prepared you for the position. Provide a brief sketch of your formal education. Be specific. Discuss relevant projects and/or specific courses that prepared you for the tasks required by the job. If you have examples of your work, take them to the interview, or provide photos of finished projects. Direct the interviewer to places that show examples of your work or to people who can provide explanations of your work. Be sure the examples are representative of your best work and are flawless. Be sure the people to whom you direct the interviewer will provide him or her with positive information about you and your work.

If you have no experience and your education is the only preparation you have for a position, explain how your course work relates to the job for which you are applying. Be willing to take an entry-level position and work your way up the ladder. An employer is impressed by a candidate who is willing to begin at the ground floor.

Do you have a list of your references with you? Why did you choose them? Be prepared for this question. Have a list of references keyed on a sheet of paper that matches your resume paper. Include the title "References for (Your Name)."

References should be people who can and will give you a glowing recommendation. Ask your references for permission to use their name, and call them before you go to an interview to let them know they may be contacted. Provide them with a brief description of the position for which you are applying, including required skills they know you possess. If you have not been in contact with your references for a while, remind them of who you are and what you accomplished so they can refresh their memories. References want to provide good recommendations if they can; therefore, give them the information they need to do their best for you.

- **Work Style**

How do you manage your time? Explain how you prioritize, schedule, and analyze tasks to develop a work plan or schedule. Emphasize your organizational skills and task management techniques. Employers are searching for employees who use time and resources effectively to accomplish the tasks required of a particular position.

Are you task-oriented or concept-oriented? You must provide a balanced answer. You want to sound versatile and able to accomplish a task, but you want to show you can come up with ideas as well. Give examples of ideas you developed and tasks you completed. Your answer does not need to be a lengthy one; just provide evidence of your performance relating to both task and concept orientation.

Describe how you identify and then solve problems. If you are not aware a problem exists, then obviously you can make no effort to solve it. Employers seek people who can solve problems; but they also need problem identifiers. Do not mistake this for the whiners and complainers in a company who always find fault. Problem identifiers are those who know a problem exists and accurately define the problem. Problem solvers are those who can find a solution to an identified problem.

This question also requires a balanced answer. Employers are looking for people who can identify and solve problems. Most employees know when something is wrong. Some employees can tell the employer that a problem exists and identify the problem. The employee most valued by an employer knows that a problem exists, defines the problem, and provides a possible solution to the problem. This is the message you want to convey to the interviewer. You are both a problem identifier and a problem solver.

Describe a situation in which you worked on a team project. What was your contribution to the project? The more challenging and complex the project and the more people on the team the better. Be able to describe concisely the purpose of the project and the team and your responsibility to the team. Describe the contributions you made that helped the team complete the project effectively and on time. Emphasize the prioritizing, task management, time management, and communication skills you used in completing your responsibilities, resulting in a positive outcome of the project.

Do you prefer to work alone or in a group? The best answer to this question is "It depends on the project or task." Many times team efforts bring new and better solutions to problems. Some tasks can be more efficiently and effectively completed by one person. The employer is looking for an employee who can be both an effective team player when the task requires it and a person who can produce quality results when working alone. It is important to convey the message clearly that you can do both.

What would you change about your current job? Tackle this question with caution. Avoid saying negative things about your current position, supervisor, or company. The interviewer may assume if you are willing to discuss your current situation negatively, you will do the same with your next position. You also do not want to indicate that you would not change anything. The interviewer would then ask, "If everything is so good with your current position, why do you want to leave?" Therefore, concentrate on your growth and desire for a challenge. Indicate that you have outgrown the job or have a desire to expand your responsibilities. Explain how you view this new position as an opportunity for professional growth and as a challenge you are willing to meet.

Describe a time when you made a bad decision. You are being forced to describe a negative situation. Prepare yourself by focusing on a decision you made based on inexperience or lack of sufficient information that produced negative results. Demonstrate how you have chosen to use this bad decision as a learning experience to develop better decision-making techniques.

- **Company Knowledge**

What do you know about our company? Here is your opportunity to demonstrate that you did your homework by researching the company. Give a thumbnail sketch of the company's product, give an overview of its mission statement, and describe its market and its competitors. Be sure this portion of your answer is brief. Continue by describing what challenges you see the organization facing in the future, and briefly and enthusiastically describe why you are interested in working for the company.

Why do you want to join our organization? Do not discuss what benefits you will derive. Focus on the skills and abilities you possess that will enhance the mission of the company. You may discuss the reputation of the company or the challenges of the industry that appeal to you. You could describe a positive encounter you experienced with the company or its product.

Why did you apply for this job? Discuss the positive things about the company/ industry that interest you. Demonstrate how you can contribute positively to the future success of the company.

- **Interpersonal Relationships**

How would your supervisor (coworkers/friends) describe you? Develop your answer based on which of the three relationships is selected by the interviewer. Answer the question using a minimum of three terms the interviewer would consider to be positive from the relationship point of view. For example, the supervisor might say hard-working, ethical, competent; the coworker might say a team player, resourceful, a problem solver; friends might say fun, caring, loyal. No matter which relationship you describe, the terms would relate positively to the workplace.

- **Career Aspirations/Professionalism**

Where do you want to be in 5, 10 or 15 years? The employer is looking for a person who sets goals and has some idea of where and what he or she wants to be. Focus your answer on areas that would benefit both you and the company. Discuss educational goals, skill development, and interests you would like to explore. Do not discuss interests in positions or job titles that are unrelated to the job for which you are applying. The interviewer will eliminate you immediately.

For example, it would not be wise to say, "I plan to open my own business in the near future." This conveys to the employer that you are interested in the job to gain whatever skills you lack to open your own business and then you will leave. Most employers are looking for long-term employees.

What goal have you currently set to help you attain your five-year goal? From your answer to the previous question, set a realistic, specific goal that would be a first step in the process. Suppose your goal is to obtain an M.B.A. degree in five years. Your first step would be to apply to a college or university and enroll in a class. This demonstrates to the employer your determination and dedication to the goals you have set.

Describe your ideal job. In describing your ideal job, be sure to closely match the job you describe to the job description of the one for which you are applying. Discuss the skills and strengths and the expected contributions you will make to the company.

Tell me about your salary expectations. Be prepared for this question by researching salaries of other comparable positions in the industry. You may be able to use published salary scales. The classified newspaper ads may give you some indication. Trade or union publications may also give you some clues. The most effective source, however, is your network. The result of your research should provide you with a salary range.

In order to give an educated answer to this question, you must have some information about benefits the company offers. If benefits have not been discussed, preface your answer with an explanation of the impact that a benefits package would have on your answer. Then request an explanation of the company's benefits. The more benefits a company offers that you would not have to provide for yourself, the lower the salary range you request may be. Benefits packages may add thousands to the actual dollar value of a salary. Benefits may come in the form of medical/dental insurance, life insurance, retirement funds, stock options, and more. More specific strategies and techniques for handling this question will be discussed in Topic 8, "Strategies for Negotiating the Deal."

Why do you want to leave your current job? Refrain from speaking negatively about your current position, supervisor, or company. You may be viewed as a potential problem causer, thereby eliminating yourself from consideration for the position. Two good reasons for leaving a job are personal growth and situations that are beyond your control.

Personal growth or the desire to obtain a more challenging position is a viable reason for seeking new employment. These motivators are not necessarily negative reflections on your current employer, but they are positive reflections on your personal commitment to challenge yourself by utilizing your talents for self-improvement.

Situations that are out of your control are also good reasons for leaving a position. Perhaps the plant or company is laying off due to economic conditions or changes in the market. This situation certainly could not be blamed on you. Perhaps the department in which you are working is being phased out due to changes in the demands of the company. Again, you would not have caused this to occur. Even the relocation of a spouse's job could be considered a situation out of your control; however, a spouse's potential for frequent moves may have a negative effect on a potential employer.

If you are leaving your current position for reasons other than the two stated previously, you must be able to explain adequately to the potential new employer your efforts to make the situation work with the current employer. If you are leaving your current position because you have been asked to resign or have been fired or your reasons for leaving are negative, you must be able to explain those reasons to your interviewer and describe what you have done to correct the problem. Topic 6 will cover this issue extensively—"Strategies for Handling the Tough Questions/Obstacles."

Interview questions and the length of the interview vary depending upon the purpose. A screening interview is usually short and the questions more focused on job skills and preparation because the interviewer's purpose is to determine if you meet the minimum qualifications. Hiring or selection interviews are longer and include more questions due to the critical nature of the information needed by the interviewer to make a wise decision in hiring.

A Comprehensive List of Frequently Asked Questions[1]

The comprehensive list of questions that follows includes the most commonly asked questions by 95 percent of all interviewers. Familiarize yourself with them. Be prepared to answer any of them during the interview process.

Questions Relating to Your Interest in the Company and the Job
- How did you learn about this position?
- Are you familiar with our company?
- Why are you interested in our company?
- Why do you think you are qualified for the position?
- Why do you want this job?
- What is the ideal job for you?

Questions Regarding Your Ability to Do the Job
- What are your greatest strengths?
- What is your major weakness?
- Why should I hire you?
- If I talked to your former employer, what would the person say about you?
- What in your last job did you enjoy the most? Why?
- What in your last job did you enjoy the least? Why?
- If I talked with your former colleagues, what would they say about you?
- What can you tell me about yourself?

Questions Regarding Education
- Why did you choose your major area of study?
- What was your academic average in school?
- What honors did you earn?
- In what extracurricular activities were you involved?
- Which courses did you like the best? the least? Why?
- How have the classes that you completed as part of your major helped you to prepare for your career?

Questions Regarding Your Ability to Fit into the Organization
- If you disagreed with something your supervisor asked you to do, what would you do?
- What type of work atmosphere do you prefer?
- Is a sense of humor important at work? Why or why not?
- Tell me about a conflict you have had with someone. How did you handle that conflict?
- What is your definition of diversity?
- How do you handle pressure?
- How would your previous employers and coworkers describe you?

Questions Regarding Experience
- Have you ever been fired or asked to resign from a position?
- Why did you leave your previous job?
- Have you had any problems with previous supervisors?
- What are your greatest strengths?
- What do you not do well?
- Why should I hire you?
- What salary do you expect?

The Salary Question. As addressed earlier, you should have an idea of an appropriate salary before going to an interview. You may check the Internet or job advertisements of your local paper for salaries in your area. Your placement office is another good source for local salary information. Handling the salary issue will be discussed extensively in Topic 8, "Strategies for Negotiating the Deal".

RECAP OF KEY CONCEPTS

- Interviewers will ask about personal interest and character, skill preparation and qualifications, work style, company knowledge, interpersonal relationships, and career aspirations/professionalism.

- When answering interview questions, you should be aware of the reasons behind the question and strategies for answering the questions. Since you are the most qualified person to talk about you, make your answers good.

- The comprehensive list of interview questions is a good guide to use to prepare for any type of interview. The more familiar you are with the commonly asked interview questions, the better prepared you will be in a true interview situation.

3
Interviewing Styles

AT THE CORE
This topic examines:

> ➤ INTERVIEW METHODS
> ➤ THE PURPOSE OF INTERVIEWS
> ➤ INTERVIEW FORMATS AND STRUCTURES
> ➤ ACING THE SECOND INTERVIEW
> ➤ INTERVIEWING PITFALLS

Strategy #3: Your attitude is a reflection of how you look at things, whether it is a glass of water, a job, or an interview. Your performance can depend on your attitude. Be sure it's positive.

Interviews fall into a variety of styles. They have different purposes, different formats or structures, and different methods. Each interview must have an established purpose, a selected method of getting the information needed, and a chosen format or structure within which the interviewer will operate.

Interview Methods

Formal/Directed Interview. During a formal, or structured, interview, the interviewer asks the same or similar questions of each candidate. The questions are planned prior to the interview and usually follow the same sequence. This style is used to keep the playing field level, assuring equal treatment of each candidate. The types of questions vary from those requiring one- or two-word answers to open-ended questions, which require more thought and the ability to articulate effective answers. As with all questions, listening and eye contact are very important.

Informal/Discussion Interview. An informal, or discussion, interview is a conversational exchange between the applicant and the interviewer. The questions asked are usually open-ended questions that require more than a yes or no answer. For example, the interviewer may describe the position, then ask you to describe your ideal job or the skills you possess that would enable you to do the job. Because it appears to be a conversation or discussion rather than an interview, do not become too relaxed and too forthcoming with opinions. It is still an interview. The questions in this style of interview may not be the same with each candidate. The interviewer may allow the interview to take a different path, depending on the answers given by a candidate.

©PhotoDisc, Inc.

The Purpose of Interviews

All interviews do not end in the hiring of an applicant. Some interviews are preliminary, some are targeted to gain specific information, some are designed to determine the behavior of a candidate when placed in a contrived situation, and others are the final step in hiring.

Screening Interview. The screening interview is a preliminary exploration of your skills and abilities to see if you meet the minimum qualifications for the position. The interviewer is often a member of the human resources department of the company. The questions will be directed specifically at your skills and abilities to see if you meet the minimum requirements for the position. In addition, the interviewer may look for personality traits and/or attitudes that indicate whether you would be a "fit" for the company. To prepare for this type of interview, do your homework. Know what the company needs. Prepare yourself to sell the skills you have that match the needs of the organization. These interviews may put you on the company's shortlist for further consideration or eliminate you from the search.

Selection, or Hiring, Interview. The selection, or hiring, interview is usually the final interview. Members of the department in which the position exists or personnel from the organization who will work closely with the successful candidate often conduct the interview. This type of interview is more investigative of how the applicant will perform on the job if selected for the position. Most questions are open-ended to determine whether the applicant is a possible fit with the organization. The style of the interview is discussion.

Stress Interview. The stress interview is used to put the applicant on the defensive to establish how he or she handles negative and/or hostile situations. Applicants for high-stress jobs (such as aggressive sales jobs and high-contact customer service center positions) are candidates for this type of interview. The type of questioning or the environment is deliberately made uncomfortable for the job seeker. The questioning may be argumentative and combative. The interviewer may disagree with what you say almost to the point of being rude. The interviewer will attempt to fluster you. The temperature in the room or the seating may be uncomfortable. All of this is created to see how well you hold your own in adverse conditions. Strategies to assist you in this situation include keeping a clear head. Keep your composure, even though you are not told ahead of time what you are going to experience during your interview. Remember that the interviewer is not angry with you. Listen carefully. Answer confidently. Remain tactful, polite, unruffled, and diplomatic.

Interview Formats and Structures

Interview formats vary widely, and some interviews may even utilize more than one format.

One-on-One Interview. The one-on-one interview is what immediately comes to mind when the word *interview* is mentioned. In this situation, one interviewer questions one interviewee. The one-on-one interview is typically used in a small company, such as a single-attorney law firm, a small medical practice, an insurance broker's office, or a small retail store. Larger companies with more employees, especially where employees interact with each other, often use the panel, or team, interview format. Strategies for effectively handling one-on-one interviews include maintaining good eye contact; being prepared to share your knowledge of the company and to discuss your career plans, goals, and experience; and displaying enthusiasm.

©PhotoDisc, Inc.

Panel, or Team, Interview. The panel, or team, interview consists of a group of four to eight panel members who conduct the question-and-answer session with the candidate. A lead interviewer is usually appointed to facilitate the interview. The leader should meet with the panel in advance to establish the questions to be asked, the order, and the general organization of the interview. The leader should conduct the introductions and initiate the interview. A description of the position, which then leads into the questioning, is an effective way to begin the process. The leader should also summarize and conclude the interview.

Although most interviews are uncomfortable, the panel interview seems to be more intimidating than the one-on-one interview. Facing four to eight pairs of eyes all focused on you is rarely a comfortable situation. Eye contact is very important, however. As each panel member poses a question, your eyes should be on that person. If possible, note the names and positions of each member. You may be able to answer questions more effectively if you tie in the responsibilities of the position to the questioner's position.

On-Site Interview. Traditionally, job interviews take place at the job location or within the company facility. They may be held in an office or a conference room. Take advantage of the opportunity to observe the corporate climate. Are people friendly and welcoming, or are you ignored as you walk through the facility? Observe the ergonomics of the facility. Does the physical plant present a pleasant work environment? Notice the employees. How are they dressed? Do they present a professional image? Do you sense that they have pride in the company and their positions? Are the physical surroundings well maintained? Are shrubs trimmed, is the grass cut, and are sidewalks edged and clean of litter? Much can be learned about a company during your interview visit, just by observation.

Your observations may also give you information to use during the interview. You may have the opportunity to mention the friendliness and helpfulness of the employees or the impressive physical structure. Make a complimentary remark to the interviewer; as long as the statement you make is true, it will not appear to be false flattery.

Off-Site Interview. Your local chamber of commerce or your college may sponsor a job fair. Employers are invited to come to a central location to set up booths and meet with job seekers. Employers have the opportunity to meet many skilled people who are looking for positions. Job seekers have the opportunity to meet employers who are looking for the skills they possess without going through the letter-writing and application process.

As a job seeker, take a lot of freshly printed copies of your resume to give to the employers you meet. If an interview opportunity occurs during the job fair, you must try to shut out the noise and confusion around you to focus on the interviewer and the questions being asked. Listen carefully to the questions. Maintain good eye contact, as it may help you hear the questions over external distractions.

An interviewer may travel from his or her home base to interview you in your surroundings. The interview could be held at a local hotel/motel conference room, a local branch office of the company, or a restaurant. All the strategies mentioned previously apply to this situation as well.

Meal Interview. The purpose of a meal interview is to observe how an applicant conducts himself or herself in a social situation. An attorney who was considering hiring a recent graduate as his new administrative assistant took her to lunch. He believed she needed to be able to handle herself in social situations with clients, and this was one way to test her skills. It is not unusual for upper-level management job interviews to include a social situation. Some strategies for success include the following:

- Wait to be seated, unless the host states otherwise, until the host and the remainder of the attendees are present.
- Place your napkin in your lap.
- Do not smoke or drink alcohol even if others do.

- If you leave the table for any reason, excuse yourself and leave your napkin on your chair.
- Use your knife and fork to consume your meal unless you are eating a finger food, such as a sandwich.
- Order something that is easy to cut and eat. For example, order a boneless chicken breast rather than chicken on the bone.
- Do not let used utensils touch the table or tablecloth. Even the handles of a knife and fork should not touch the table.
- Do not leave a spoon or fork in a cup or bowl. It should rest on a flat dish. This is why cups have saucers and soup bowls are served on plates.
- Between bites, rest the knife horizontally across the top of your plate and rest the fork horizontally across the center of the plate.
- Do not request a to-go box or bag for food you did not eat.
- When you are finished, rest your knife and fork on the plate at the four o'clock position. The blade of the knife should be facing you.
- At the end of the meal, place your napkin on the table next to your plate. Do not refold it or place it in your chair.

©PhotoDisc, Inc.

At the end of the meal, express your appreciation for the meal to your host. Within 24 hours, write a thank-you note for the opportunity to learn more about the job, to learn more about the company, or to meet prospective colleagues over a meal.[1]

Videotaped Interview. Videotaped interviews do not occur often, but they are worth mentioning. They are useful for higher-level management positions. The situation may occur when members of an interview team are not available or when a company would like to screen individuals before the executives of the company become involved. The company may hire a service provider to videotape the interview. Then the video can be viewed as many times as necessary at the convenience of the interview team or by the company's decision-making executives. This method is also effective if distance and travel expense is a consideration.

Effective strategies to consider when interviewing via videotape are the same as those mentioned in Topic 1 for videoconferencing.

Be sensitive to what you wear. The rainbow effect and distortion can affect the quality of the videotape and, therefore, be a distraction to the viewer. Avoid flashy or noisy jewelry. If you have prepared notes for the interview, keep the shuffling of papers to a minimum, as the sound may become amplified. Although it may be disconcerting and intimidating, maintain good eye contact by keeping your eyes on the camera.

Sequential Interviews. For many positions, especially upper management, more than one interview may be required. Sequential interviews are a set of interviews where a decision is made after each whether to continue the interview process with the candidate. A successful candidate will return for additional interviews; the unsuccessful candidate will receive notification that no more interviews will be held. Usually, the interviews are one-on-one but with a different person each time. However, be prepared if you have a team, or panel, interview; a previous interviewer may be one of the team. These interviews most likely occur on different days because the purpose is to screen the candidates in or out.

The sequential interview is primarily a series of screening interviews to narrow the pool of candidates. Strategies for successfully interviewing in a sequential interview are to consider it an opportunity to learn more about the company, to take advantage of the chance to ask questions in subsequent interviews that you forgot to ask in the initial interview, and to continue to demonstrate your value as a potential employee.[3]

Serial Interviews. Serial interviews consist of several interviews one after the other. With serial interviews, the series is set up from the time the first interview is scheduled and no decision is made until all the interviews have been completed. Usually, each meeting is with a different group of people, and all interviews are held over a one- to two-day period. Following the interviews, the individuals or teams you met will get together to compare notes and make a collective hiring decision.[4]

As an example of a serial interview, consider the hiring of a college president. The morning may hold three different interviews. It may begin with a breakfast interview with vice presidents of the college, be followed by a meeting with the officers of the faculty senate, and end with a meeting of the academic deans. Lunch may be with selected faculty. The afternoon may be an interview with the business affairs division of the college, followed by a meeting with the student services officers. A reception then may be held for the entire college to meet the candidate, followed by dinner with the board of trustees or commission.

The strategy here is to treat each meeting as your first interview. Keep in mind that for the interviewers, it is their first meeting with you. Try to keep your answers fresh and enthusiastic. Each group will have its own concerns and interest in your abilities and its own expectations of what is needed. Seek to determine what it is the interviewers want in the ideal candidate. You job is to show them you have what they want and need.

> **TIP**   During serial interviews, treat each interview as if it were your first.

Acing the Second Interview

You have been called to return for a second interview. You obviously made a positive first impression. You must have presented yourself successfully the first time around. Your goal now is to give a repeat performance. You will be meeting more and different people. It may take longer and be in the form of a serial interview. You will probably have the opportunity to meet upper management, potential peers, and your supervisor. A meal could be included in this scenario.

The focus of these interviews is "Can you do the job?" and "Can you work with us?" Your strategy is to convince the various individuals and groups with whom you meet that you have the experience and competence to do the job and the compatibility to get along with coworkers and superiors. Tony Michaels, manager of Organizational Planning and Development at Burlington Industries, suggests the strategy of acquiring more than a cursory knowledge about the company. "We're impressed by candidates who have networked with our employees or student interns to learn more about who we are, what we do, and what the job would entail," says Michaels. "That confirms their interest in working for us, which influences our hiring decisions."[4]

Interviewing Pitfalls

It pays to research a company and prepare for questions concerning your career plans and goals. In 2001, Accountemps[SM][5], the world's largest temporary staffing service for accounting, finance, and bookkeeping professionals, conducted a survey of 150 executives with the nation's largest companies. Accountemps discovered that 44 percent of employers believe the most common deficiency among job candidates is that they have little to no knowledge about the company with whom they are interviewing. With the availability of the Internet and the massive amount of information it offers, it seems impossible that nearly half of all job seekers do not use this readily available resource to boost their chances for a job.

Max Messmer, chairman of Accountemps and author of *Managing Your Career for Dummies* says, "The more information candidates have about potential employers, the better prepared they will be to demonstrate this knowledge during the interview." He points out that prospective employees should be able to answer the following key questions before meeting with a hiring manager:

- What business is the company in?
- What products and/or services does it sell?
- Who are its primary competitors?
- What current industry issues or events are of interest to the firm?
- What are the company's mission, vision, and values?[6]

Be sure you research and find answers to these questions before you go to your first interview.

The second most common mistake job seekers make during interviews, according to the survey, is the lack of preparation to discuss career plans and goals. As Yogi Berra once said, "If you don't know where you are going, you might end up somewhere else."[7] Know what you want to do and where you want to go, and be prepared to discuss it at the interview.

RECAP OF KEY CONCEPTS

- In a formal/directed interview, each candidate is asked the same or similar questions; in an informal/discussion interview, the interviewer may take a different path, depending on the answers given by a candidate.

- Each interview should have a defined purpose. A screening interview is to determine if a candidate will be considered further for a position. The selection, or hiring, interview, usually the final interview, is to determine if a person is the right fit for a position. The stress interview is to determine how a candidate will perform in a negative and/or hostile situation.

- Interviews formats and structures vary widely. Interviews often incorporate more than one format in the same interview. They may be one-on-one or team/panel; they may be on-site or off-site. They may be held during a social situation, such as dinner or lunch. They may be videotaped. For upper-management positions, they may be sequential or serial.

- Acing the second interview may simply require you to repeat your previous performance. The focus of the second interview is "Can you do the job?" and "Can you work with us?"

- The biggest interview pitfall made by job candidates, according to an Accountemps survey, is having little or no knowledge about a company. The second biggest mistake made by job candidates is lack of preparation to discuss career plans and goals.

4
Strategies for Planning, Preparing, and Practicing

AT THE CORE
This topic examines:

➤ **WHAT AN EMPLOYER WANTS**

➤ **IF YOU ARE THE RIGHT FIT**

➤ **NECESSARY DOCUMENTATION**

➤ **THE RIGHT IMAGE**

➤ **PREPARING THE RIGHT ANSWERS**

➤ **GETTING TO THE INTERVIEW ON TIME**

> *Strategy #4: "Most people who fail to get the job they really want fail not because they are not qualified but because they failed in the interview. And most failures occur because they aren't prepared."*
>
> **—David W. Crawley, Jr.[1]**

K nowing what an employer wants and showing the employer you have the "right stuff" are critical to a successful interview. Certain documentation will be required to prove that you have the "right stuff." Within seven to ten seconds, the employer will make a decision based on his or her first impression of you, so you want to project the right image through the power of self-presentation and nonverbal communication. What you say and do in the interview will determine your place on the employer's shortlist. Be sure you make the list by answering questions effectively and behaving appropriately during the interview. Display interest and enthusiasm for the position by getting to the interview on time.

What an Employer Wants

Before you can project what an employer wants, you must learn what that is in a prospective employee. What the employer wants is what the employer needs. It is your task to discover these needs. You must determine if you have the skills, talents, and abilities for which the employer is searching. Several methods can be used to discover if you meet the employer's requirements. If the employer has advertised for a position, a job description must be available. The job description should provide an insight into the skills required for the position.

Check the company's web site, the company's human resources department, personal networks, college placement offices, newspapers, public employment agencies, private employment agencies, temporary employment agencies, professional organizations, the local chamber of commerce and/or Better Business Bureau, trade journals, and magazines.

In addition, study the company's web site to gather as much information about the company as possible. Request any brochures the company has. If possible, obtain a copy of the company's newsletter, which may contain valuable information for your search. Read the company's mission statement to determine how it sees itself in relation to its market.

The most important sources of information about the company are not in hard-copy format, but in your career network, which is composed of those individuals connected to you through your career field. Someone in your network will have information about the company you are researching. Try to find someone who is currently working for the firm. If possible, interview this person to learn as much as you can about the company. Perhaps you can get an insider's view of the position for which you are applying.

The results of your research should provide you with enough information about the company and the position to give you an advantage in the interview. Compile a profile of the company. Once you know the company's focus and needs, you can provide evidence that you can meet those needs. Of course, all of this is based on the premise that the employer has carefully determined what the needs of the company are.

Victor Kiam told of the time a young man wanted to work for him at Remington™. After looking over the applicant's resume, Kiam told him there wasn't anything available. The young man refused to end the interview. He said, "I think there's an opening for me, but I don't know where it is yet."

He offered Kiam a plan. He would work for 30 days without compensation, wagering his free labor that he'd find a position for himself at Remington. Within the 30 days, he found some problems and outlined how he would solve them. He got the job.[2]

In this case, Mr. Kiam, the employer, did not even know what he needed.

> **TIP** To get hired, you may have to sell someone on the idea of how much he or she needs you.[3]

Are You the Right Fit?

The following factors may be used to determine your fitness for an organization:

- **Define yourself.** You must know who you are. You must assess your strengths and weaknesses. Compile a list on paper, and assess your values and abilities. List the things you value or think are important. List specific abilities you have, such as software knowledge, certifications or licensures, and so on. From this list, compile a profile.
- **Create a personal mission statement.** The statement should define who you are, why you exist, and what you will do to become the person you want to be. Your mission statement should be based on your value system. Write your mission statement on a card and carry it with you. Refer to it often. It will be your guide through life and help bring you back to center when you stray from your goals; it will serve as a reminder of the person you are working to become.
- **Determine the corporate culture.** Every company has a corporate culture. It is the environment of unwritten rules of behavior and values that influence the way business is conducted in the

workplace. The more you can learn about a company's corporate culture before an interview, the better prepared you will be to answer the questions you are asked. More importantly, this knowledge will enable you to ask questions that yield the additional information you need to make a good decision about a job offer.

©PhotoDisc, Inc.

- **Comparing profiles.** You have completed a personal profile describing your strengths, weaknesses, values, and abilities. You have a similar profile of the company. Compare and contrast your profile against the company's profile. Do any areas match? Do you have similar values? Will your strengths prove useful to the company? Will the company prove useful to you and meet some of your needs and help you reach your goals?

- **Check your attitude.** Attitude may be the single most important ingredient that will enhance your interviewing skills. Your attitude must be positive, which can display self-confidence, self-assurance, interest, enthusiasm, energy, and capability. Employers are looking for employees who are dependable, creative, future-oriented, and interested in the well-being of the company. Positive people can meet those expectations.

"Our performance can depend on our attitude."

—Tom Landry, Football Coach

There is no room at the interview table for negativity. Negative people are not future-oriented or interested in what is best for the company. Rarely are negative people creative, due to the dark cloud under which they operate. A negative person can be depended upon only to complain or criticize. A negative person does not move a company forward one inch; it is the positive person who helps move a company forward. Therefore, check to be sure your attitude is positive.

Initially at the interview, you display your positive attitude in nonverbal ways. You display your attitude through your facial expressions, by the way you walk, by the way you greet the people you meet, by your handshake. Be sure to smile. Walk with your head erect and a bounce in your step. Walk quickly and with assurance that you know where you are going. Not only does this display a positive attitude, it also presents an air of confidence. Greet the people you meet with a warm smile and a firm handshake; repeat their names if possible. All these elements are characteristic of self-confident, positive people —the types of people employers want to hire.

- **Acquire Needed Skills.** Once you determine the skills the employer wants the new employee to possess, assess your skills. Do you have what you need? Lacking a particular skill the employer wants does not mean you should not apply for the position. For example, if the employer states in the job description that a master's degree is required and you possess only a bachelor's degree, examine your resources and determine how you can obtain the required education. Be prepared to explain to the interviewer the plan you have implemented and the approximate time you have allotted to acquire the degree.

Apply for a position only if you have most of the qualifications for the position. If you are unqualified, you are wasting your time and resources and those of the employer.

Necessary Documentation

When you begin the job search, gather the appropriate documentation you may need or the employer may request. Being prepared helps you avoid stress and frustration.

Resume. Of course, you will need your resume. Be sure you have updated all the information and the resume is flawless. Be sure all information provided about your education and work experience is accurate and truthful. Later disclosure that information provided is not truthful may lead to dismissal. Print an original copy to take with you to an interview in case the interviewer requests a copy.

Job Application Form. If you have not previously completed an application form, call the company to have one sent to you or make a special trip to the company to complete one. Many companies now make applications available on their web sites, in which case you can key the application. This is a small detail that is so important in making an effective, positive first impression. Check the application carefully for typographical errors before printing it. As with the resume, all information provided must be truthful and accurate.

A young man was selected as a town's new fire chief. After three years in the job, it came to light that the chief had been arrested for arson when he was seventeen years old. He was immediately fired. He was not fired because he was arrested at seventeen for arson. He was fired because he did not tell the truth on his job application. Dishonesty, even in the form of omission, may lead to dismissal.

References. Compile a list of references to supply to your interviewer should you be asked. Select a minimum of three. A variety should be included from educational instructors, work-related supervisors or coworkers, and personal friends who know you and know of your work. Do not choose relatives or people who do not know you well enough to give you a glowing recommendation.

Transcripts/Certifications. If you have minimal or no experience, obtain a transcript of your college work if your grades are good. This does not have to be an official transcript that you take with you to an interview; it can be one that has been issued to you by the college or university. However, some organizations require official transcripts be sent directly to them. Do not tamper in any way with a college transcript, even if it is unofficial. Doing so is grounds for dismissal if it is discovered later that the transcript did not accurately display your college work. If you have any certifications or licensure for specific skills, take a copy of the documentation with you to an interview. Be willing to leave a copy with the interviewer for later reference. Do not give him or her the original.

Social Security Card/ID Card. Always take your original social security card with you to an interview. If you do not have an original, make a trip to your local social security office to obtain one.

It will take a few days to a couple of weeks to get the card, so plan ahead. Be prepared; get the original before you need it. Employers must see the card, and it must be the original. Employers may also ask for a picture ID. A driver's license is usually adequate. If you do not have a driver's license because you do not drive, contact your state's motor vehicle department for a nondrivers ID card.

Prepared Questions. Toward the close of the interview, the interviewer usually asks if you have any questions. It is best to be prepared with some formulated questions before entering into the interview. Prepare five to eight questions. Remember, in the course of the interview, the interviewer may answer one of your prepared questions; therefore, think before you ask, and have more than one question from which to choose.

All the documents you create must be flawless. Perfection is your goal in this situation. Be sure your documents are printed on quality paper with a laser or ink-jet printer. They will speak volumes to the interviewer and assist in creating a positive impression. Take the time and opportunity to create a positive, professional impression.

The Right Image

> **TIP** At the interview, your goal is to convince the employer that you are the right person for the job.

Projecting the right image includes your total presentation. This means the outside and the inside. Your outward appearance includes from the top of your head to the tip of your toes. The four main attributes of a professional image include:

- Appropriate professional appearance.
- Use of correct manners and etiquette.
- Appropriate personal behavior.
- Effective communications.

Appropriate Professional Appearance. Professional appearance is a composite of your professional dress and your grooming. The message communicated is the result of a combination of these two factors. Professional dress can be defined as dressing in such a manner as to enhance your authority, promote your respect, aid in your promotion, and promote your advancement opportunities in the workplace. Professional dress involves appropriate clothing selection based the following considerations:

- Profession
- Company policies on dress
- Level of customer and client interaction
- Geographic location
- Clothing care and maintenance
- Appropriate styles for your individual body
- Types of functions you must attend
- Budget and purchasing techniques

You can see from the list that achieving an appropriate professional appearance requires time and careful thought. Personal grooming habits are also important in enhancing your professional image. You must develop and practice good grooming habits to ensure that your appearance is always clean and polished in your professional role. Grooming involves all aspects of your body, including the following:

- Hair
- Nails
- Teeth
- Makeup[4]

When you begin the job hunt, invest in a good haircut. Then keep it in shape as necessary. The first thing a person notices and can describe about you is your hair. Keep it clean and conservatively styled during the job-hunting process. Avoid an unusual color and unconventional styling.

In addition, either get or give yourself a good manicure. Your hands are visible appendages and are noticed when you shake hands or when you hand the interviewer your resume or references. For men, nails should be clean and cut short and straight across. Cuticles should be smooth and pushed back. For women, nails should be clean, short to medium length—the tips should be no longer than a quarter inch. Polish is acceptable, but use a clear, light pink, or pale tan color. Nails should not attract attention, but should complement the rest of your professional look.

©PhotoDisc, Inc.

Facial grooming includes shaving for men and makeup for women. For men, it is acceptable to have a beard or mustache or other facial hair. Be sure it is well-groomed and clean and any shaven parts of the face are freshly shaven for the interview. For men who choose to be clean-shaven, be sure you shave before the interview to avoid a five o'clock shadow.

For women, makeup should be understated and have a professional look. Avoid a heavy layered look. If possible, put makeup on just before leaving for an interview so you have a fresh appearance. You may choose not to wear makeup. If so, be sure you have cleansed your face well and applied a good moisturizer.

To complete your grooming before an interview, if you wear glasses, clean all parts of them well. Take a bath or shower. Use deodorant. Use minimal or no cologne, aftershave, or perfume. Brush your teeth.

TIP Do not use mouthwash. Mouthwashes often contain small amounts of alcohol, and the last thing you want included in the interviewer's first impression is the scent of alcohol on your breath.

Dress. Ten to twenty years ago this was an easy decision to make. For both men and women, the answer was a navy blue suit, a white blouse or shirt, and black shoes for men and navy pumps for women. Men wore a dark red or navy tie with a small, discreet pattern. Women wore simple jewelry, such as pearls and small pearl earrings. Why navy? According to *The Complete Idiot's Guide to Successful Dressing*, dark colors suggest authority, and dark blue conveys the greatest degree of authority.[5]

Today the rules have relaxed somewhat, and the classic interview outfit has changed. In fact, sometimes it is difficult to determine what is appropriate; it then becomes industry-dependent. An established conservative firm may still expect the navy blue power/authority look. Computer software companies are renowned for their casual approach to workplace dress. In companies where creativity is essential, a very conservative look may put you at a disadvantage. Whereas in a very conservative company, anything different from the norm may be inappropriate.

Your research becomes very important. Ask someone you know who works at the company or someone in your network who might have knowledge of what is appropriate to wear. Whatever your final decision, your ultimate goal is to present a serious, professional look.

The most formal, conservative look is the solid-colored suit, white shirt/blouse, black shoes and socks for men, and matching shoes and hose for women. Shirts, blouses, suit jackets, dress jackets, and dresses should be long-sleeved. Appropriate jewelry for women is simple—small earrings (no larger than a quarter, not dangling) with a simple gold or pearl necklace. Limit the number of rings worn to a wedding band/engagement ring. If you are unmarried or not engaged, a small unobtrusive ring or none would be appropriate. Men should wear a dark red or navy small-patterned tie. Socks should be upper-calf to knee length so no skin shows when you are seated.

In a less conservative firm, colors may be added. The monochromatic look that is popular now for men (shirt, tie, and suit the same or similar shades of the same color) is appropriate. Women may wear a plain, solid-colored suit or long-sleeved dress.

In a more casual firm, it is still not appropriate to wear denim to an interview. Do not be that casual. But to this interview, men might choose to wear a sport jacket and pants of contrasting color with a colored shirt and an appropriate tie. Women might choose to wear a solid-colored pantsuit or blazer and contrasting skirt. Shoes should be appropriate. Men can wear brown loafers if they match the color of the pants. Women should choose pumps in a color that matches her selected pants or skirt.

Clothes do not have to be expensive to look good, but they do have to look good to create a positive first impression. When you are shopping for an interview outfit, spend the extra time and money necessary to be sure the item you have chosen fits properly. It should not be too tight or too loose or too long or too short. Walk around the store in it. Sit down in it. Is it comfortable, or are you pulling at it? Be sure to look at it from the back. Although you would not see it from the back, the interviewer and other people will. Check the back and sides as well as the front. Men should wear a long-sleeved shirt with a suit and wear an undershirt beneath the shirt. The suit and shirt will fit better, maintain their shape, and stay in place.

What about a briefcase and/or purse? For women, make a decision for one or the other, not both. The last thing you want to do when arriving for an interview is to juggle a purse and briefcase while trying to shake hands. Carry the documents you want to take with you to the interview in a black or navy pocket folder, a leather-bound notebook, or a briefcase. A purse can be left in the trunk of the car.

Finally, make sure your interview outfit is ready to put on at any time. Be sure the shirt or blouse is clean and pressed, the suit is spotlessly clean, the shoes are polished, and the hose/socks have no holes or runs. (For women, it is a good idea to carry an extra pair of hose with you to the interview, just in case!) You should have the external parts ready at any time an interview is scheduled.

Attitude. Now it is time to look at the internal attributes that are an important part of preparing for the interview. I recently saw a woman who was wearing a T-shirt that read "Attitude is everything." Denis Waitley, in *The Psychology of Winning*, describes the ten qualities of a total winner. As he discusses positive self-expectancy, he says, "The most readily identifiable quality of the total winner is an overall attitude of personal optimism and enthusiasm. Winners understand the psychosomatic relationship that the body expresses what the mind is concerned with. They know that life is a self-fulfilling prophecy, that a person usually gets what he or she actively expects."[6]

Mr. Waitley is one of many saying the same thing. If you believe you will succeed, you will; and if you believe you will fail, you will. A positive, optimistic, enthusiastic attitude is a winning attitude. You display your attitude by what you say, the way you say it, the way you walk, the way you stand, and the way you sit because it is the way you think.

Unfortunate situations may occur that cause you to develop a negative attitude. Perhaps you lost your job because the company downsized due to conditions in the marketplace. You certainly were not to blame, but you may feel angry and bitter because of your perceived unfairness of the situation. If possible, take time to deal with your anger and bitterness before starting a job search. Do the best you can to put the experience behind you because your feelings will show in your interview, resulting in being rejected for the position and adding more fuel to your anger and resentment. It is easy to say but very important to remember that anger and bitterness are self-defeating emotions. They do little to move you forward and do much to hold you back.

©PhotoDisc, Inc.

> *"I firmly believe that the only disability in life is a bad attitude."*
> **—Scott Hamilton, Olympic Gold Medalist 1984**

In 2000, Accountemps completed a survey of 1,400 chief financial officers in which they asked what the most valued interpersonal skills were in accounting candidates today. Thirty-eight percent responded "positive attitude."[7] Success in careers today requires more than just the top skills in your field. It also calls for a positive attitude and enthusiasm for work.

TIP Before you leave for an interview, check your attitude. Visualize success and be optimistic about the outcome of the interview.

Self-Confidence. Your self-confidence is directly related to your own estimate of your self-worth, or the value you assign to yourself as a human being. Like attitude, self-confidence displays itself in everything you do—how you meet and greet people, how you shake hands, how you formulate and deliver ideas, and how you carry yourself as you move from place to place. Self-confidence is positive self-esteem and a positive sense of self-worth. This does not mean being self-centered, but it does mean genuinely liking yourself and having an appreciation of your talents.

With self-confidence, a positive attitude, appropriate clothing, and good grooming, you are headed for the winner's circle in the interview. These four aspects of your initial interview presentation will make the right first impression on the interviewer. In the interview, they will give you the confidence and self-assurance you need to do your best.

Manners and Etiquette. Your professional image is also communicated through your use of appropriate manners and etiquette. It is important to be familiar with the different protocols of behavior as they relate to social manners and etiquette. Some of these include the following:

- Making introductions and greetings
- Being able to initiate and maintain conversations
- Respecting the customs of others
- Being able to express appreciation
- Knowing appropriate dining rules and protocol
- Extending courteous behavior to others
- Knowing how to behave in difficult situations

Manners and etiquette are important in the overall professional image you project. You can learn to be competent in these areas and enhance your professional image by practicing the etiquette requirements for different situations.

Most people feel comfortable once they know what is required and how to meet those expectations. Many resources are available to help you develop this aspect of your professional image.

TIP Your personal behavior also communicates a message about your professional image.

Personal Behavior. As a professional, you want to be the type of person who practices a code of personal behavior that demonstrates respect for your organization and the people who work with you. You should recognize that personal behavior contributes to the overall professional image you project. Some aspects of personal behavior include:

- Respecting the organization and its rules.
- Being a loyal employee.
- Conducting business in an ethical manner.
- Assuming responsibility.
- Respecting the diversity of people.

Each of these aspects of personal behavior is very important in the business world, and your reputation for your commitment to these will be established early in your career. You should give careful attention to personal behavior. Many people have been high achievers and projected an appropriate image in their appearance, yet failed in their career because they did not take responsibility for their personal behavior.

Communications Skills. Another significant component of your professional image is your ability to communicate effectively with others. Communication should be clear, concise, and accurate. You communicate verbally and nonverbally in the business world. Nonverbal communications send messages about your professional image. These nonverbal communications include the following:

- Posture
- Facial gestures
- Neatness
- Listening
- Personal behavior
- Punctuality

For example, a person who is always late may not say "I don't respect your time," but that is certainly the message that is communicated through this nonverbal action. In addition to nonverbal communications, effective verbal communication is very important. Verbal communication includes:

- Correct pronunciation and enunciation when speaking.
- Appropriate written communications.
- Expression of written appreciation.
- Effective listening.
- Effective verbal communication in difficult situations.

The ability to communicate effectively can be developed and refined as you progress through your career. Give significant attention to the development of these skills. They will contribute to your professional image and help determine the level of success you attain in your career.

Preparing the Right Answers

Part of the preparation that goes into interviewing is preparing answers to questions the interviewer will ask. Research possible interview questions. There are many books and web sites that provide examples of questions you might be asked. The questions fall into several general categories. Topic 2, "Frequently Asked Questions" includes a comprehensive list of the more commonly asked questions and provides strategies for answering the top 25.

Develop Effective Answers. Your next goal in the preparation phase of interviewing is to prepare effective answers to the questions. You want to plan ahead. You may not have a ready answer for all the questions, but if you have some ideas in mind to help you develop effective answers, you are in a good position to experience a successful interview.

Introductory questions are icebreakers, usually designed to put you at ease and give you an opportunity to use your oral communication skills. Be able to describe yourself from a career perspective and to demonstrate your research on the company.

Questions about your skills and abilities examine specific qualifications for the job. Make a personal assessment of your abilities of both hard and soft skills. Determine your strengths, and look closely at your weaknesses.

Work/education questions inquire about experiences that have prepared you for the position. Review your education and your work history. Be sure you can articulate what you learned and can describe your responsibilities in previous jobs. Look for what you liked best and least in both school and work. How did you work and study?

Questions concerning your interpersonal relationships are becoming frequent as teamwork and workplace conflict become more important. Determine how you interact with others. Consider taking the Myers-Briggs Type Indicator or another inventory that will help you learn more about how you center your attention to the world of people, things, or decisions. You can check with your college counselor or human resources department. Either should be able to direct you to someone who can assist you.

Some questions may require you to examine your leadership skills and style of management. Be prepared to discuss characteristics of a good leader and to provide examples of your leadership/management experiences; focus especially on the tough issues.

Finally, most companies are looking for a well-rounded person who is enthusiastic and has an avid interest in life. An interviewer wants to hear about interests you have outside the workplace (such as hobbies, volunteer activities, sports—spectator or participatory, and so on).

Practice Your Answers. Once you have the questions, develop the answers; then practice. Practice but do not memorize. Try practicing the "Tell me about yourself" question in front of a mirror. Have a friend role-play as the interviewer and ask you some questions. Practice as you are driving to work or school. Adopting this strategy will help you gain confidence by organizing your thoughts. Practice will give you a sense of preparedness.

Getting to the Interview on Time

You have an interview appointment. Your attitude is positive. You have gathered your documentation. Your image is appropriate and professional. You are confident you have effective answers to the questions. Now you must get to the interview on time. It is possible to overcome most problems that arise during an interview, but rarely can anyone overcome being late.

A week or so before the interview, determine the location and approximate travel time. Practice the drive or ride, whatever your mode of transportation. Look for possible obstacles. To avoid late buses or trains, take an earlier one. To avoid traffic problems, leave earlier than the approximate travel time required. Even if you arrive 20 to 30 minutes early, do not enter the company until 10 to 15 minutes before your scheduled interview time. Use your extra time wisely by observing the grounds and buildings.

If due to some unusual circumstance you will be late, call immediately to inform your interviewer of the situation and approximate time of delay. If you know it will be impossible for you to get there at all or your arrival will be greatly delayed, ask if the interview can be rescheduled. Do not be surprised, however, if this has a negative impact on your interview and chances for the job.

RECAP OF KEY CONCEPTS

- To project what an employer wants in an employee, you must research to determine the employer's needs/wants. Use the job description, the company's web site, the company's human resources department, your college placement office, employment agencies, and so on.

- To determine if you are the right fit for an organization, you must define yourself, create a personal mission statement, and determine the company's corporate culture. Then compare yourself with the company, check your attitude, and acquire any needed skills.

- Collect the documentation you need to take with you to the interview—resume, job application form, references, transcripts or certifications, social security card, ID card, and questions you will ask the interviewer.

- Project the right image by checking to see that your professional appearance is appropriate. This is a composite of your professional dress and your grooming. Other important parts of projecting the right image are attitude, self-confidence, manners, personal behavior, and communication skills.

- Research typical questions for the interview; then practice appropriate and effective answers.

- Get to the interview on time. Make a trial run; then expect the unexpected, and leave early.

5
Strategies for Impressing, Expressing, and Egressing

AT THE CORE
This topic examines:

➤ STAGES OF THE INTERVIEW

➤ MANNERS AND NERVE CONTROL

➤ STRATEGIES FOR EFFECTIVE VERBAL AND NONVERBAL COMMUNICATION

> Strategy #5: "I'm turned off by people who haven't done their homework."
>
> **—Donald Kendall, Chairman, Pepsico™** [1]

Y ou have an appointment for an interview. Your clothing is appropriate, clean, pressed, and ready to go. Your attitude is positive, and you are feeling self-assured. You have collected all the necessary documentation, researched the company, and practiced answers to possible questions. You arrive on time; you are ready! Let's examine what you might encounter as you meet your interviewer.

Stages of the Interview

Most interviews follow a similar structure. There are six stages: meeting and greeting, the warm-up, interviewers' questions and your answers, your questions, the summary and the conclusion. By understanding the stages, you can approximate where you are and anticipate and prepare yourself for the next stage. Knowledge of the process and procedures can also help to relieve your anxiety and nervousness.

Stage 1: Meeting and Greeting. During the meeting-and-greeting stage, introductions are made. If the interview is face-to-face and the interviewer offers his or her hand, take advantage of this opportunity to display self-assurance with a firm, confident handshake. Listen carefully to the names and positions of any interviewers. Repeat the names as you shake hands with each person. If there is more than one interviewer and the opportunity is presented, you may jot down the names of the interviewers to reference throughout the interview.

> **TIP** You may ask for the interviewers' business cards so you can refer to them during the questioning.

During this meeting-and-greeting stage, conversation may be general with various topics covered, such as the weather, local events, and travel to the interview. These are icebreakers, and the attempt is to provide a more comfortable environment for the interview. Experienced interviewers know they will learn more if the applicant is relaxed; therefore, an attempt is made to create a pleasant atmosphere.

Stage 2: The Warm-up. During this stage, a good interviewer gives you a description of the position and its responsibilities. Listen carefully to develop effective questions to ask when the opportunity arises and to provide job-directed answers to questions. Again, an effective interviewer will attempt to establish rapport by asking questions that help to ease some of the stress you are experiencing. He or she will ask a question or two just to help you relax.

A typical first question is an opened-ended question such as "Tell me about yourself." This can take a variety of formats, but essentially the interviewer wants to observe your oral communication skills. You should be prepared to explain who you are on a professional/career level.

- Think only about what has prepared you for this position. Do not discuss personal issues such as age, children, family, or religious affiliation.
- Limit your response. Prepare a brief description of your education and previous jobs—just a line or two about each. You will be asked about your previous experiences in depth later in the interview.

- Tell the positive stuff since this is the beginning of the sales job.

Stage 3: Interviewers' Questions and Your Answers.

Questions can be divided into two categories: closed-ended and open-ended. Closed-ended questions require a yes or no or one- to two-word answer. For example, "Have you had any experience with handling difficult customers?" Open-ended questions require the applicant to use communication skills to relate a situation and solution to the interviewer. For example, "Describe how you handled a difficult customer." Both types of questions have value, and the applicant should be prepared to answer both.

You will be asked questions about your work and educational history and to discuss the information you have supplied on your resume and/or job application form. If there are gaps in time or you have job-hopped, be prepared to explain why and what you did during those times. If your educational history is relevant, you will be questioned about the experiences that prepared you for the position. Experience often weighs heavier with an employer than education, but do not underestimate the effect of a degree or certification. Stress the advantages and assets that would be available to the company if you were hired.

Next, your skills will be examined. The investigation will question both your hard and soft skills. Hard skills include your computer knowledge, oral and written communication strengths, knowledge of and ability to operate equipment or machinery, and so on. Soft skills are your interpersonal skills, such as teamwork, customer service, leadership, decision-making, and problem-solving skills. Be prepared to answer questions concerning your strengths and weaknesses in both areas. When discussing your weaknesses, include how you plan to improve. For example, "I am not yet at the expert level in Microsoft Access, but I have enrolled in a course at the local college and plan to take the MOUS certification exam within six months."

Another strategy for handling the weakness question is to discuss a problem the employer would view as a positive. For example, "Sometimes I find myself pushing for perfection when I know it is more important to strive for excellence because perfection is an unrealistic goal." The terms *perfection* and *excellence* will fall positively on the employer's ears. Your statement will also ring positive bells because you have defined your understanding of the difference between the two.

Stage 4: Your Questions. Once the interviewers establish that your qualifications and experiences have prepared you for the position, they will move on to the next stage of the interview, which normally is the time for your questions. This is your chance. Do not hesitate to take advantage of the opportunity.

TIP   When the interviewer asks if you have any questions, the only correct answer is yes.

You should have established some questions to ask the interviewer during your interview preparation. Do not pass up this opportunity to ask important questions that could help you come to a decision about your employment with the company. You also want to be sure the questions you ask are appropriate for the level of the interview.

If you are in your first interview, you want to learn as much about the company and the position as possible. This is not the time to discuss benefits or money. Good questions to ask in the first round are about job content, the company's culture, and future plans.[2]

Eliminate any questions if the subject was covered during the preceding stages of the interview. You certainly should request clarification of any position responsibilities about which you are unclear or confused. What you need to gather at this point is enough information to make an informed decision if the job is offered to you.

Remember, an interview is an exchange of information. The company is trying to determine if you have what they need. You must also decide if the company has what you need.

It is also important to consider the interviewer and his or her position. The human resources person is likely to know about job descriptions, qualities being sought, and morale or company culture. The manager who is hiring, your potential supervisor, is the person who can answer questions about the department, the team with whom you will be working, and the challenges of the job.[3]

When do you ask questions about benefits, vacation time, work schedule, stock options, and salary? You do need this information to make an informed decision about working for the company. As the interview process evolves, the appropriate time will come to ask these critical questions. You also may be able to obtain a pamphlet or brochure from the human resources department.

What you should *not* ask during the
first round.

- Do not address the benefits issue.
- Do not ask any questions that were
  answered during the interview.

©PhotoDisc, Inc.

What questions should you ask
during the first round of interviews?

- May I see a copy of the job description?
- Why is the position available?
- What qualities are you seeking in the candidate for the position?
- What is the next step in the hiring process?
- When are you anticipating making a decision about the position?[4]

Prepare before your question time. List four to six questions
that would be appropriate. Take into consideration the level of the
interview and the position of the interviewer. Demonstrate that you
are a person who does the research and is prepared for the occasion.

This is an ideal time to offer the interviewer a list of your
references. You will demonstrate your preparation and willingness to
provide a list of people who can supply positive and glowing recommendations. Be sure the list contains a minimum of three references.
Give names, positions if they are business or educational references,
complete business addresses, and phone numbers. If they are personal
references, provide names, addresses and phone numbers. You might
even want to add the number of years you have known each person.

Stage 5: Summing Up. During this stage of the interview, it is
the interviewer's responsibility to provide you with information about
what process and procedure will be used to notify you when a decision
is made. You may have already received this information if you asked
questions about the process during your question time. If the interviewer should attempt to skip this stage, initiate a summary of your
understanding of the position and request an explanation of the
decision-making procedures.

Although you may be feeling a sense of enormous relief that the
interview is coming to a conclusion, continue to listen carefully. You

want to know what you can expect from the company. How soon do they anticipate filling the position? How far along are they in the interviewing process? When will they make their decision? Take notes if possible.

If the interviewer does not request that you call with any more questions, it is perfectly acceptable to ask whether you can do so. A good strategy during the summing up stage is to be very clear about what happens next. How will they inform you of the decision? Will they call, write, or e-mail you?

Stage 6: The Conclusion. The interviewer will indicate in some way that the interview is concluding. Often the interviewer will stand or ask if you have any more questions, offer a handshake, and thank you for coming to the interview. At this point, stand, shake hands, and thank the interviewer for his or her time and consideration. End with a statement such as "I look forward to hearing from you."

> **TIP** Suggest the interviewer call if you can provide any additional information that will help him or her make a decision.

Then gather your things together and leave. Do not linger. If you are not sure how to exit the facility easily, request directions. If you exit through an office in which the administrative assistant or someone else provided you with assistance on your arrival, thank the person for his or her help. This is good etiquette and will be noted by the individual who helped you. He or she might tell someone else that you expressed your gratitude for the assistance. Your simple act may move you to the top of the list. When competition for a position within a company is stiff, the person who pays attention to details and goes one step further often gets the offer. You want that person to be you.

Manners and Nerve Control

Most interviewers understand that an applicant is nervous. The interviewer might even find it a negative if you are not a bit nervous. A little nervousness can be beneficial. A little tenseness can sharpen your acuity and awareness. The negativity of nervousness comes when it interferes with, rather than enhances, your performance.

The most important strategy to use when dealing with nervousness is preparation. Barbara Walters offers this advice to prospective interviewees: "My best advice for dealing with destructive anxiety is homework . . . homework helps enormously when you apply for a job."[5] Homework includes researching the company and the position, perfecting your professional image, polishing your manners, practicing answers to questions, and getting to the interview on time.

A second strategy that often helps with nervousness is to reverse your focus. Rather than zeroing in on yourself and how you will do, focus on the employer and what he or she needs.[6] This reversal of thought may help you relax about your performance as you turn your thoughts to the employer.

Another reversal of focus is to think of the interview as an information-gathering process. It is a necessary process to determine if you are good for the company and the company is good for you. Take the pressure off yourself by changing your focus from one of need for acceptance to one of need for information.

> **TIP**   Change how you think about the interview process. Focus on the employer and his or her needs, or think of the interview as an information gathering process.

As the interview approaches and you become nervous, your heart rate increases, your mouth becomes dry, and your palms become damp and sticky. The nearer the time approaches, the more pronounced the symptoms become. Why do these signs of nervousness occur? They occur due to fear—fear of rejection.

A technique to overcome fear and nervousness is to determine what is the worst that could possibly occur. The worst that could possibly happen is that you do not get the job. You must consciously realize that not being selected is not the end of the world. There will be another day and another job interview, so change your perspective. The job may not be the right one for you anyway. If you were not selected, you probably were not right for the company; therefore, the company was not right for you.

A third strategy for handling nervous symptoms is to employ some calming techniques.[7] The best calming technique is effective breathing. Take deep breaths by inhaling through your nose and quietly exhaling through your mouth. With shallow breathing, you take very little oxygen into your lungs: therefore, very little rich oxygenated blood gets to the brain, which it needs to function at its best. Take five or six of these deep, cleansing breaths.

> **TIP** Preparation is the secret to an effective interview and relief from pre-interview stress.

The second calming technique is as simple as the Boy Scout motto of "Be Prepared." Do you remember a time when you went to school unprepared to take a test? You had not studied and were not ready to answer the questions on the test. You felt anxious, your heart rate increased, your hands got moist and sticky, and your mouth got dry. This reaction is similar to the anxiety preceding an interview for which you are not prepared. Contrast this with a time you went to school prepared to take the test. Your confidence was calming. Anxiety did not come into play because you had studied and were prepared to take the test. The same is true in preparing for an interview. If you know you have practiced and you are confident of your answers to the most common questions, you are more self-assured and, therefore, have less fear of rejection.

Good Manners Make Good Impressions. Knowledge of appropriate behavior in any situation is also a technique for calming the nerves. Manners can give you a sense of security and ease the anxiety of being in an unfamiliar environment. Because you have the confidence of knowing when to stand, sit, shake hands, and say please, thank you and can focus on the information and the positive image you want to convey.

When you arrive in the room where the interview is to be held, do not sit until your interviewer either indicates where you are to sit or requests that you sit. Sit up straight in the chair toward the front edge of the seat, and lean forward slightly. This simple technique conveys interest and involvement in what is occurring. By placing your feet flat on the floor with one foot slightly ahead of the other, you relieve stress on your lower back. Do not slouch in the seat.

Control nervous habits. If you are holding a pen, do not click or cap and uncap the top or tap it on the table. Do not pull at your coat or skirt bottom or lapel. Do not shuffle papers. Place your hands quietly in your lap or on the table.

Strategies for Effective Verbal and Nonverbal Communication

Unless you are interviewing by telephone, your verbal communication and what you are communicating through body language will be evaluated. Everything counts.

Articulation and Enunciation. Be conscious of your enunciation and articulation. Hold your head erect, and speak directly to the listener. Do not mumble. Take a few seconds to formulate your answers to questions before you begin speaking. Do not ramble. Practicing answers becomes invaluable.

Handle Silence Effectively. As a society, we are not comfortable with silence. Have you ever noticed when food is served at a dinner how silence often falls over the table when people begin eating? Invariably someone will make a comment about how food is more important than conversation to this group. Because people are uncomfortable with silence, they have a need to fill it with sound. An experienced and effective interviewer will use silence to observe how you handle the discomfort. Let silence be your friend. Do not try to fill the silence. If you do, you will most likely get into trouble by saying more than you want to. If the silence goes on longer than you find comfortable, you might ask if the interviewer would like you to expand on your answer.

Body Language. Body language conveys many messages and may or may not be interpreted correctly by the receiver. Be sure the messages you send are clear. Some nonverbal strategies to assist you in conveying an effective and positive message are as follows:

- Maintain eye contact with your questioner.
- Show a positive attitude by smiling. A smile invariably brightens your face and communicates confidence.

- Display interest and enthusiasm by sitting on the end of your chair. Lean forward slightly. By combining this with appropriate eye contact, you are conveying eagerness to listen and learn.

©PhotoDisc, Inc.

Eye Contact. Maintaining good eye contact with your interviewer indicates that you are a keen listener. Although you do not want to stare at the interviewer, you want to look at the interviewer most of the time. Try moving your eyes from the interviewer's right eye to his or her left eye or from the center of the forehead to the end of the nose. Looking off occasionally may indicate you are thinking, but always look at the interviewer while he or she is talking.

During your interview, you have three goals. First, you want to create a positive first impression. Impress your interviewer by your appearance, your self-assurance, and your poise. Look as though you can handle anything that comes your way. Your second goal is to express yourself effectively and to convince your interviewer that your qualifications are just what the company needs. Get the interviewer to like what he or she sees and hears. Your final goal is to exit the interview, leaving a picture in the interviewer's mind of a professional, capable, and qualified potential employee that he or she wants to hire.

RECAP OF KEY CONCEPTS

- The interview generally follows a routine pattern of six stages: meeting and greeting, warm-up, interviewers' questions and your answers, your questions, summing up, and the conclusion.

- During the meeting-and-greeting stage, introductions are made. Try to remember names and positions.

- In the warm-up stage, the interviewer attempts to establish rapport with the interviewee. Think about your preparation. Keep your descriptions brief but accurate. Tell the positive stuff.

- Interview questions take two formats: closed-ended and open-ended. The questions will be about your work and educational history. Your skills will be examined.

- Stage 4 is your opportunity to ask questions of the interviewer. When the interviewer asks if you have any questions, the only answer is yes.

- Summing up is the next stage. You should learn what process and procedure will be used to notify you of a decision. If the procedure is not explained, ask.

- At the conclusion of the interview, express your appreciation for the interviewer's time and the opportunity to interview. As you leave the company, thank anyone who assisted you.

- Controlling nervous tension is important. One strategy is to change how you look at the interview process. Think of it as an information-gathering process. The second strategy is to employ calming techniques. Utilize effective breathing techniques, and be prepared by practicing for the interview.

- Both verbal and nonverbal communication skills are critical to the success of an interview. Articulation and enunciation are important. Handle silence effectively. Use body language to convey a positive attitude and enthusiasm. Maintain good eye contact with your interviewers.

6

Strategies for Handling the Tough Questions/Obstacles

AT THE CORE

This topic examines:

➤ **ILLEGAL QUESTIONS**
➤ **STRATEGIES FOR DEALING WITH ILLEGAL QUESTIONS**
➤ **STRATEGIES FOR DEALING WITH OBSTACLES**

> *Strategy #6: Anticipate questions and their intent, and then plan your answers.*

Title VII of the Civil Rights Act of 1964 prohibits discrimination on the basis of race and sex in hiring, promoting, or firing. The Equal Employment Opportunity Commission (EEOC) was created to implement the law. Subsequent legislation expanded the role of the EEOC to enforce laws that prohibit discrimination based on race, color, religion, sex, national origin, disability, or age in hiring, promoting, firing, setting wages, testing, training, apprenticeship, and all other terms and conditions of employment.[1] This topic will discuss the implications of interview questions in the hiring process as it relates to the Civil Rights Act of 1964.

In addition, some of the obstacles you may face in any given interview will be discussed. Such obstacles include age, quantity of experience, being fired or laid off, gaps in your work experience, and job-hopping. This topic offers strategies to assist you in clearing those obstacles.

Illegal Questions

You might be asked illegal questions during the interviewing process. Therefore, it is important to understand what the illegal topics are and how questions can be phrased that makes them either legal or illegal.

Race and Sex. Title VII of the Civil Rights Act of 1964 makes it illegal for anyone to ask questions during the hiring process that would force an applicant to provide information concerning race or gender. Although in a face-to-face interview these factors might be obvious, it is illegal for an interviewer to ask such questions. If there is a specific job-related reason to obtain this information, it is legal to ask about gender or race. For example, if a modeling agency requires a black male for a photo shoot, the interviewer may ask questions concerning race and gender because it is a requirement of the job. However, it could be difficult to prove that only a black male meets the requirement when an Asian, white, or Hispanic male could also be used in the shoot.

> **TIP** Personal questions considered to be job-related usually are allowed during the interview or on the job application.

Age. The Age Discrimination Act of 1978 prohibits discrimination against applicants forty years of age or older.[2] Interviewers may ask if you are over eighteen because there are legal implications. However, they may not ask any question that would attempt to illicit your age or date of birth. They cannot ask when you graduated from high school because your approximate age can be determined by the year of your graduation.

Health and Disabilities. The Americans with Disabilities Act (ADA) of 1990 prohibits discrimination based on mental or physical disability as long as those disabilities are not directly related to job performance. Even then, if reasonable accommodations can be made to enable you to perform particular tasks, you cannot be discriminated against.[3]

Interviewers can ask if you are able to perform the job. However, they may not ask about your state of health or that of your family, whether you have had any surgeries/illnesses or plan any surgeries, or if you have any disabilities. If you do have a disability but it will not interfere with your ability to perform the responsibilities of the position for which you are applying, you are not required to inform the interviewer of the disability.

> **TIP** "Can you perform the job's essential functions with or without reasonable accommodations?" is a legal question.

Marital Status/Children/Pregnancy. The Pregnancy Discrimination Act prohibits discrimination in hiring or the employment of pregnant women or women with pregnancy-related medical conditions.[4] The interviewer cannot ask if you are married, what your spouse does, if you have children or the ages of your children, if you are pregnant or plan to become pregnant, or what child-care arrangements you have made. They can ask if you have problems with specific conditions of the position, such as working hours, travel, and so on.

National Origin/Ancestry/Parentage. The Immigration and Control Act of 1986 prohibits the employment of illegal aliens, but also protects against discrimination of legal aliens based on national origin or citizenship status.[5] Interviewers may not ask any questions concerning your ethnicity. They cannot ask where you or your parents were born or what native language you speak. They can ask if you are proficient in a foreign language, but only if it is relevant to the performance of the job for which you are applying. They may not ask if you are an American citizen. However, they can ask about paperwork necessary for employment in the United States.

Religion/Political Beliefs/Nonprofessional Affiliations.
Interviewers may not ask questions about your religion, your beliefs, or what clubs or organizations to which you belong. They may not inquire about what place of worship you attend or whether you attend. They cannot ask about your religious beliefs even if you are applying for a

position in a house of worship unless the performance of the job requires certain beliefs, such as may be required of a minister, rabbi, priest, and so on. They cannot ask what religious holidays you observe. They cannot ask if your religion permits you to work on a particular day of the week. However, they can explain that the job requires work on Sunday, then ask if that is a problem.

They cannot ask what political preferences you have or if you belong to any organizations or clubs unless they are asking about professional organizations that are relevant to the position for which you are applying. For example, an interviewer may ask an attorney if he or she is a member of the American Bar Association or a local bar association but can not ask if he or she is a member of a local country club or associated with a local, state, or national political party.

Physical Appearance. Interviewers may not ask questions concerning physical appearance although this information is obvious at a face-to-face interview. Height and weight cannot be asked unless the job requirements for performance demand a minimum or maximum height or weight. For example, minimum and maximum height and weight requirements are set for jet fighter pilots due to the size of the cockpit. In this case, it is legal to inquire about height and weight because less than minimum height/weight or excessive height/weight restricts the person's ability to perform the job successfully.

Other Restrictions. Interviewers cannot ask if you are in debt or how much you owe or if you rent or own your own home. They cannot ask if you have ever been arrested unless it is for a specific crime and it is job-related. However, if you are required to handle money in the performance of a job, they may ask about your arrest record.

Strategies for Dealing with Illegal Questions

Interviewers should know what is legal to ask during a job interview; however, many do not. As a result, you may be asked an illegal question. How should you handle it? Think carefully about what you would do before you are put in the position of having to answer an illegal question. Basically, there are four strategies from which to choose. The one you select may depend on what is most important to you.

1. Answer the question. If you really want the job and the principle does not concern you, then answer the question. It may not concern you if the employer knows you are married and have three children. In truth, interviewers may not even realize that a question is illegal and their purpose in asking a question is not for discriminatory reasons. They may be asking because they are truly interested in you as a person and are attempting to learn more personal information to determine if you will be a good "fit" for the company.

©PhotoDisc, Inc.

2. Deflect the question. You may choose not to answer the question directly. Suppose the interviewer asks what native language you speak. You might ask politely, "May I ask how this question is related to the position for which I applied?" This may deflect the interviewer from pursuing his or her line of questioning, or the interviewer may state that an applicant who speaks Spanish has an advantage in this job. You can then reply that you speak, read, and write Spanish fluently. You have stated that you are fluent in the language but have not revealed any knowledge of ethnic background, national origin, or citizenship.

You may also choose to deflect the question with humor. Suppose the interviewer asked, "How tall are you?" You could respond by stating, "Well, I have never had a problem getting on any of the rides at Disney World." You have said that you are over 4 feet tall. Or if the interviewer asks if you are married, you could reply that you feel as though you are married to your career because of the time and effort and love you have for your profession. You have not answered the question and have subtly indicated to the interviewer that you are not going to answer it.

3. Deal with the concern behind the question, and ignore the illegal question itself. The interviewer asks, "Do you have children?" If your choice is to answer the question, try to determine why the interviewer has asked the question. Your answer is "Yes, I have two children. Johnny is seven, and Melissa is five. If your concern is child-care arrangements, both children are in school and I have them enrolled in an after-school program."

Often the employer is concerned about absences from work, particularly for women who have small children. By explaining that you have arrangements for the children, you have alleviated some of the employer's concern. The concern of child care is almost exclusively focused on women. Men would never be asked about child care unless the interviewer knew the man was a single father. Discriminatory? Absolutely.

An interviewer asks a female candidate "Do you plan to have children?" This is an illegal question. An appropriate answer might be "Whether or not I plan to have children in the future is not really relevant to my career. I plan to work and have a career no matter what happens in my personal life."

The interviewer is asking this because he or she wants to make sure you are the solution to the problem, not the source of more headaches. When the female candidate is asked about her plans regarding motherhood, the interviewer may be trying to determine whether she is in for the long term or just until the company pays for the birth of a child. It is clearly a discriminatory question, one that would probably not have been asked of a male candidate, and it is illegal.[6]

4. Refuse to answer the question. Your fourth option is to openly refuse to answer the question by asking "How are my political views relevant to my performance on this job?" It is not necessary to be hostile, but it is essential that you let the interviewer know you find the question offensive and discriminatory. If you refuse to answer the question, you will probably not be offered the job. In all probability, you would not be happy in that environment anyway.

An applicant for a secretarial position was asked if she were a born-again Christian. Although the employer assured the applicant it was not a requirement for hire, the applicant chose not to pursue the position. She believed that if the interviewer asked an illegal question and did not know it was illegal, then in all probability, there were other breaches of employment practices occurring in the business.

You may choose any of the four strategies for handling an illegal question, but you should be comfortable with your choice. Consider carefully the consequences of each of the options. If you believe you have been discriminated against in one of these areas, you have two options. One, you can ignore it and move on. Realistically you probably would not be happy working in an environment where discrimination is an issue. Two, you can pursue the discrimination in the legal arena. The first step to pursuing it legally would be to contact an attorney that deals with employment issues to see if you have a case. Consider carefully the consequences of this with regard to the expense of time, energy, and money. The EEOC processes approximately 48,000 claims annually.[7]

Strategies for Dealing with Obstacles

You may face one or more obstacles to your success during the interviewing process. An employer may consciously or unconsciously make a hiring decision based on your age: too old or too young. Your experience and qualifications may influence an employer's decision negatively: too much or too little. Being laid off or fired are two other obstacles that may impact on your success. Two obstacles you must be able to explain are gaps in your work history or evidence of job-hopping. The following strategies may help you eliminate the employer's concern about these issues.

Age: Too Old, Too Young. Even though it is a violation of the Age Discrimination in Employment Act of 1967, to discriminate against anyone who is forty or older, you may believe you are at a disadvantage because of your age. You may assume the employer will think you are too young or too old for the position. You want to dispel his or her concerns during the interview.

If you are older and believe your age will be a disadvantage in your pursuit of a particular position, distract the interviewer's focus from your age to your experience. Emphasize the work experience you have had in the field, and de-emphasize your age. Discuss the skills you have that are applicable to the position. Emphasize your maturity and stability. If your children are grown, point out that your parenting responsibilities are minimal and will not interfere with your commitment to the responsibilities of the position.

If you believe your youth may be a factor in your being hired for a particular position, it is as important to emphasize your skills and experience as it is for older applicants. By focusing your attention and, therefore, the interviewer's attention toward the talents and abilities that qualify you for the position, you divert the interviewer's mind away from your age. Emphasize your enthusiasm, energy, and positive commitment to responsibilities of the position. Display enthusiasm for the company, its product, and its position in the market. Relate a positive experience you have had with the company's product. Age will disappear as a factor in the decision making.

Experience: Too Much, Too Little. What if you are over-qualified for a position? You must convince the interviewer you are the person for the job and emphasize how much you will bring to the position because of all your experience. Emphasize your skills and your commitment to giving 100 percent to whatever jobs you hold. Employers know that the break-in period for any position is expensive, and the sooner an employee is working at maximum performance, the better. Therefore, emphasize your confidence in your ability to step right into the job with very little training.

TIP Remember, the person with the most education, the most experience, and the best qualifications does not necessarily get the job.

The applicant the interviewer likes best usually gets the job. Therefore, if you have minimum experience, you want to display enthusiasm about the position and the company. Discuss successful experiences you have had with the company's product. Emphasize your skills that will directly affect your performance in the job. Get the interviewer to like you.

Laid Off or Fired. Because self-esteem and self-worth are involved, questions concerning being laid off or fired are difficult. If you have been laid off due to downsizing or elimination of a depart-ment or group from a job, you were not in control of the situation. Most interviewers will understand and even sympathize. Your strategy in this case it to explain briefly what caused the layoff and be prepared to answer any questions this disclosure may generate.

TIP Be scrupulously and openly honest when dealing with the "fired" issue.

Being fired, however, is a different situation. Honesty is the only acceptable policy to follow in this case. You must be able to explain the circumstances that led to your dismissal. If you were at fault, accept responsibility. You should be prepared to answer specific questions about the incident. You should also convince the interviewer that your behavior or the cause of the firing has been corrected. If you are able to speak with the employer who fired you, ask what type of recommendation he or she would give if a prospective employer called for a reference. Many times a former employer will agree to state that you resigned rather than state that you were fired.

Whatever the circumstances, be honest with the interviewer. If he or she learns later that the circumstances were different from what you described, you could be dismissed from your new job.

Gaps in Your Work History. If you have been unemployed for a period of time and the gap shows on your resume, you must be ready to explain the cause. Most employers will understand the results of tough economic conditions or job shortages in your field. They will also understand if you were involved in training, retraining, or taking college classes.

However, if you have been job seeking unsuccessfully for several months, an employer may be more reluctant to hire you. You must be able to explain the gaps in your resume and work experience. There is an old adage that couldn't be truer: It is always easier to find a job while you have a job. If you are planning to leave a job, find a job while you are still working. It becomes more difficult to find a job if you are not currently employed.

If you are out of a job and looking for work, volunteer or take some classes to fill in the gaps in work. However you choose to explain, be honest about the gaps. Lying may catch up with you and ultimately cause your dismissal.

Job-Hopping. Employers define job-hopping as having had many jobs over a limited period of time. If your resume or job application form shows several jobs of two, four, or six months in length, be prepared to explain why you had so many short-term jobs. Job-hopping sends up a red flag to an interviewer of a potential problem employee. The employer is looking for long-term, stable, loyal workers.

©PhotoDisc, Inc.

In most cases, an employee's first six months with a company are the most costly to the employer. This is the period of time when an the employee is learning the job and not working at full capacity. If your work history includes several jobs of short duration, an employer will not want to invest time, resources, and money in training you only to see you leave before you are working at maximum capacity. You must give a plausible reason why you had jobs of such short duration.

RECAP OF KEY CONCEPTS

- If an interview question could be used to discriminate in hiring based on race, color, religion, sex, national origin, disability, or age, it is illegal.
- One of four strategies may be used when you are asked an illegal question during an interview. You may choose to answer the question, deflect the question, deal with the concern behind the question and ignore the illegal question itself, or refuse to answer the question.
- If you believe your advanced age may be a negative in the hiring decision, emphasize your knowledge, experience, and maturity as preparation for the position. If you believe your youth may be a detriment to your selection, emphasize your skills and enthusiasm for the job.
- If you are overqualified for a position, emphasize how quickly you can accept the responsibilities of the position. If you have little experience, get the interviewer to like you. Display enthusiasm for the company, the company's product, and the position. The most qualified applicant does not necessarily get the job.
- Be prepared to explain the circumstances if you have been laid off or fired due to a situation beyond your control. If you have been fired from a job, accept responsibility and be prepared to explain how the situation has been corrected.
- If you have unexplained breaks in your employment record, you must be able to explain to the interviewer why a gaps have occurred. Be prepared to provide evidence of productive activity during a gap, such as enrolling in classes or volunteering.
- If your resume displays evidence of job-hopping, you must be able to explain the circumstances to a potential employer. Employers are looking for long-term, stable employees.

7
Strategies for Assessing, Critiquing, and Evaluating

AT THE CORE
This topic examines:

➤ **HOW TO ASSESS, CRITIQUE, AND EVALUATE YOUR PERFORMANCE**

➤ **HOW TO ASSESS, CRITIQUE, AND EVALUATE A COMPANY AND A POSITION**

➤ **HOW TO WRITE A FOLLOW-UP/THANK-YOU LETTER**

➤ **HOW TO SOLVE THE CALLING PROBLEM**

➤ **THE REJECTION**

> *Strategy #7: Evaluate your performance at the interview so you can improve for the next one.*

The interview is over, but you are not finished. Although you would like to breathe a sigh of relief and move on, it is time to stop and review your performance before and during the interview. With new experiences, you cannot grow or improve as a result of that experience unless you evaluate and critique how you handled the situation. This postevaluation of your interview performance will help you prepare for the next interview.

Assess, Critique, and Evaluate Your Performance

The assessment of your performance must be completed as soon as possible after the interview. Consider using the following procedures:

• Write down the name(s) and title(s) of the interviewer(s) on paper.
• List all the questions you can remember being asked by the interviewer.

- List the questions you asked.
- Write the answers the interviewer gave to the questions you asked.
- Include the answers given to the questions you asked the interviewer.
- Write a brief description of your understanding of the job responsibilities.
- Review the questions you were asked. Place an asterisk in front of the questions you answered well.
- Underline the question you considered the toughest one to answer.
- Write a description of what you wore—suit, dress, shoes, jewelry.
- Write down a more effective answer to the toughest question you were asked.
- From the list you have, complete an evaluation form.

The following page shows a sample evaluation form. You may choose to create your own or use this one, but it is essential that you complete an evaluation. If you are a serious player in the job-hunting market, you may have multiple interviews. Memory is not a reliable tool to use when you need to review your performance, actions to be taken, and next steps in the process.

You may wonder why "My attire" is one of the categories. If you have multiple interviews with one company, you do not want to wear exactly the same thing to all the interviews. You will want to change a blouse or tie or jewelry. Therefore, list what you wear to each interview. This will also help you determine if your attire was acceptable and comfortable. Were you tugging at your tie or pulling at your skirt? Were you able to sit comfortably and forget about your clothing so you could concentrate on the questions?

Another category is "Next step in the process." You want to be certain you know what the next step is in a company's hiring process. When is the company planning to make a hiring decision? How will you be informed? This will help to alleviate postinterview nerves as you wait to hear a decision.

INTERVIEW EVALUATION FORM

Company name: _____ Date of interview:_____

Company address: _____ Phone number: _____

Position applied for: _____

Interviewer's name and title: _____

Type of interview: ☐ Initial/Screening   ☐ Second   ☐ Hiring

My attire: _____

The toughest question: _____

How I would answer next time: _____

_____

Position description:_____

What I learned about the company:_____

_____

☐ I was comfortable in what I chose to wear.

☐ I was on time for the interview.

☐ I gave the interviewer a firm handshake.

☐ I maintained good eye contact throughout the interview.

☐ I thanked the interviewer for his or her time and consideration.

☐ I sent a thank-you letter.   Date sent: _____

Summary of my performance: _____

Next step in the process: _____

How I could improve my performance: _____

What I wish I had said:_____

_____

Assess, Critique, and Evaluate a Company and a Position

As previously suggested, you should write a description of the position for which you applied and were interviewed as you understand it. Try to answer these questions:

- What are the major responsibilities of the position?
- Why is the position vacant?
- To whom would I be reporting?
- What are the qualifications for the position?
- Do I meet all of the qualifications?
- Are there any qualifications I don't have? If so, what are they?

Describe the corporate culture. Try to answer these questions:

- Was there an obvious dress code displayed by the employees I saw?
- What type of atmosphere did the interviewer create?
  - ☐ Friendly   ☐ Formal
  - ☐ Laid-back   ☐ Stiff
  - ☐ Comfortable   ☐ Tense
- How would I be evaluated?
- If there was more than one interviewer, did they seem to respect each other?
- What was my overall impression of the physical buildings and company grounds?

If you discussed salary and benefits with your interviewer, answer these questions:

- Was the salary range discussed within my requirements?
- Which of the following benefits were discussed?
  - Medical/Dental/Optical Insurance
  - Retirement/401K/Investment
  - Paid Sick Leave
  - Life Insurance
  - Expense Accounts/Car/Gas Allowance
  - Paid Vacation/Holidays/Personal Days

- Tuition Reimbursement
- Stock Options/Profit Sharing/Bonuses
- Other

From your answers to these questions, you can begin to get a general picture of the company, what it is offering, and the milieu in which the company operates. It is now time to write a thank-you letter.

Recently, I received a letter from a former student who had applied for a position as an administrative assistant to the commander of a unit on an air force base in the United States. She wrote to thank me for teaching her how to write a follow-up thank-you letter after an interview. Her new supervisor, the commander, told her after she was hired that her thank-you letter was what made up his mind to select her for the position. Something as simple as a thank-you can make a difference.

Write a thank-you letter within 24 hours of an interview. Address it to the interviewer. If it was a panel interview of more than one person, write the letter to the lead or chief interviewer. Send a courtesy copy to the human resources department of the company.

TIP The interview thank-you letter should be short—no more than three paragraphs and less than one page.

You have evaluated the company and the position for which you were interviewed. The resulting picture was a positive one, and you want the job. Indicate in your thank-you letter that you are interested in the position.

Follow-Up/Thank-You Letter

A thank you is an appropriate response to someone for his or her time and effort spent on your behalf. Even though you have expressed this verbally as you left the interview, a written thank you letter is a must.

TIP Be sure you have the correct spelling and address of the interviewers before writing the letters.

Thank-You Letter. In the first paragraph, express your appreciation for the opportunity to discuss your skills and qualifications for the position. State something positive about the interview or the company, and state your interest in the position.

In the second paragraph, you have several options. Choose one.

- Restate your qualifications for the position.
- Provide additional information about your qualifications that did not come up during the interview.
- Discuss anything you forgot to make known during the interview.
- Answer a question you believe you did not answer well during the interview.
- Explain why you want to work for the company.

In the third paragraph, thank the interviewer for his or her time and consideration of you for the position. Restate your interest in the position. Tell the interviewer how to reach you if he or she should require more information. Then restate what you understand the next step is in the process. For example, "As we agreed, I will call you next Wednesday to learn your decision" or "If I do not hear from you by Friday of next week, I will contact you to see how the selection process is progressing" or "I will contact you in a few days to provide you with any additional information you may require." Whatever option you choose for your closing line, follow through. If you state you will call on Wednesday, do it. You must do what you say you are going to do.

> **TIP**   The thank-you letter helps to keep you in the interviewer's mind.

Use the same paper you used for your resume. Key the letter. This attention to detail speaks volumes about your professionalism. Key the envelope using the same color, weight, and texture as the resume paper.

Thank-You, but No-Thank-You Letter. You have evaluated the company and the position for which you were interviewed. The resulting picture was not a positive one, and you are no longer interested in the position. You still write a thank-you letter, but in the letter, you indicate that you wish to withdraw your name from consideration for the position.

The first paragraph of the "Thank-You, but No-Thank-You" letter should thank the interviewer for his or her time and consideration of you for the position. State something positive about the interview, company, or position.

In the second paragraph, state that you wish to withdraw your name from consideration for the position. Explain why. Did you receive another offer? Did you discover an incompatibility between the position and your skills? Did you decide that you do not want to relocate? Was there a disclosure during the interview of additional responsibilities that forced you to reevaluate? Close this paragraph with something positive.

Paragraph three should conclude the letter with a simple closure: "Thank you again for your time and consideration" or "I am sure you will find the right person for the position."

Why would you write a letter if you are not interested in the position? First, it is simply good manners to thank someone for his or her time and effort spent on your behalf. By letting the person know you do not wish to be considered for the position, you have saved the individual time and effort he or she might otherwise have expended. Second, you cannot predict the future. Once the interviewer knows why you withdrew your name, he or she may take into consideration your concerns and reevaluate his or her position. Or there may come a time in the future when another position with the company might be just the right one for you.

> **TIP** Interviewers will remember you because you had the thoughtfulness to inform them early of your decision to remove your name from consideration for a position.

To Call or Not to Call

One of the most difficult dilemmas an interviewee faces in the week to ten days following an interview is whether to call about the decision. Will I appear too aggressive if I call? Will I appear too anxious? If I don't call, maybe they will think I am not interested?

What to do? If the company does not plan to make a decision for several weeks or months, there is no need to call the week following your interview. You will only frustrate yourself and irritate the interviewer.

Therefore, it is important to establish at the interview when a decision is expected to be made and receive permission to check on the decision-making process. If this has not been explained during the interview, your final questions should be "When are you planning to make a decision?" When you receive an answer, ask, "May I call you on (the date) to inquire about the progression of the process?" Establish what would be acceptable to the employer. Whatever you agree to do, do it. If you say you will call on Tuesday, call on Tuesday. Also, in the last paragraph of your follow-up/thank-you letter, include whatever you agree to do.

The Rejection

What if you receive a letter or phone call from the interviewer telling you were not selected. What do you do? First, understand it is inevitable if you are job hunting. The best advice is to be prepared and not take it personally. Never put all your eggs in one basket. Do not have only one job possibility. Do not stop interviewing for other jobs while you are waiting to hear the outcome of another interview. The best opportunity and the best position for you may be at the next interview, not the previous interview.

Write a thank-you letter for the notification within a day or two of receiving the rejection letter. You will be remembered for the courtesy. Indicate your disappointment in not being selected, but thank your interviewer again for considering your qualifications for the position. Express your continued interest in the company and your desire to be considered for future openings.

Here is an alternative procedure to follow if the previous one does not appeal to you. The following tactic may take courage, but it will give you an opportunity to grow. First, call the interviewer. Thank him or her for the consideration, and indicate your disappointment. In order to help you with your job search, ask why you were not selected. Determine if it was a lack of qualifications. What were you missing that the successful candidate had? You may learn that you need to brush up on your skills or improve your presentation.

Although rejection is a difficult process, you must prepare for your next interview. Review your interview evaluation form. Practice the questions you did not answer well. Change any parts of your attire that did not work. If your shoes hurt, find another pair for the next interview. Gather your documentation again. Your goal is improvement in yourself and your presentation.

RECAP OF KEY CONCEPTS

- Create and use an interview evaluation form. Evaluate your performance and the position in relation to your qualifications. Evaluate the company and its corporate culture. Review the major responsibilities of the position. Determine if the salary and benefits meet your needs.

- Within 24 hours of the interview, write and mail a thank-you letter to your interviewer. If you want the job, express your interest in the position. If you decide you do not want the job, request that your name be withdrawn from consideration. Use the same paper and envelope you used for your resume and letter of application. Key your letter.

- Solve the calling dilemma by establishing at the interview when a decision will be made. Determine how you will be informed of the decision. Ask if you may call at a specific time to request information about the hiring process.

- If you should receive a rejection letter from a company, write a thank-you letter in response within a day or two of receiving the letter.

8
Strategies for Negotiating the Deal

AT THE CORE
This topic examines:

➤ **STRATEGIES TO IMPLEMENT BEFORE A JOB OFFER IS RECEIVED**
➤ **STRATEGIES TO IMPLEMENT WHEN A JOB IS OFFERED**
➤ **STRATEGIES FOR MAKING A DECISION**
➤ **NEGOTIATING THE DEAL**
➤ **COMMUNICATING YOUR DECISION**
➤ **STRATEGIES FOR PREPARING FOR THE NEW JOB**

> *Strategy #8: Once you sign on the dotted line, it's a done deal. It's too late to make major changes in the agreement.*

The interview is over, and you have evaluated your performance, the position, and the company. You have decided you are very interested in the position. You have written your follow-up/thank-you letter. Now you have some homework to do in preparation for the possible job offer. You need to be prepared to make an informed decision if an offer is made.

Strategies Before a Job Offer Is Received

Before you receive an offer, you should take steps to prepare yourself for the possibility that an offer is forthcoming and for negotiating a deal that meets your expectations. You must know what your expectations are.

Determine Your Needs. You must determine what the minimum salary is for you to be able to maintain a roof over your head and all that accompanies it. Do not throw into the mix your current salary because your current job may have little to do with the new job. From your salary research, you should know what is reasonable to expect. Determine the minimum salary you can accept, and determine what amount would make you ecstatically happy if such an offer was made. Be sure the top end is a reasonable expectation given the position and your skills. (Do not set the top end at six figures if that is not realistic.) Between the minimum salary you must have and your ecstatically happy figure, you have a salary range. Between the two is a realistic expectation of what you should earn.

In addition to your qualifications, many external factors influence the amount of salary offered. The geographic location, the level of responsibility of the position, the type of industry, the value of the benefits offered, and so on, all influence the amount of the salary offer.

Consider geographic location. Even though the positions are identical, an employee in New York City, Chicago, or San Francisco will earn more than someone in Montpelier, Vermont; Independence, Missouri; or Provo, Utah—simply by virtue of the difference in the cost of living. Consider the industry. An accountant working for a manufacturing firm may well earn more than an accountant working for a nonprofit organization.

Consider the value of the benefits and perks being offered. A straight salary with no medical benefits would need to be substantially higher than an offer that included medical benefits. Medical insurance can cost an individual $700 – $900 per month.

You must make a list of those job factors that are important to you. Then prioritize the list. For example, your list may include answers to the following questions.

- Is traveling a consideration, either as a commute to work or for responsibilities of the position?
- Is the corporate culture one where I will fit in?
- Is the position a challenging one?
- Is my new supervisor a fit for my needs as an employee?
- Are my new coworkers a fit for my work style and personality?
- How stable is the organization and its industry?
- Are the benefits offered by the organization value-added to the salary?

- Is there growth potential either through skill development or promotions?
- How do I feel about the ergonomics of the office?
- What perks are associated with the position?

If other factors are important to you, be sure to include them on your list. Then you must prioritize each item as to level of importance. Perhaps being happy at work is your most important priority; therefore, your supervisor, coworkers, and physical office are more important to you than your optimum salary. Perhaps money is the No.1 issue to you, and you would be willing to commute the 1 1/2 hours to work or add more travel to your work schedule. This prioritized list must be dynamic; it must be changeable as you weigh all the factors in making your decision.

This list should be created before a job offer is made because it may be time-consuming to construct. You will need to refer to your previous research about the company and your interview evaluation to gather some of the information.

Strategies to Implement When a Job Is Offered

TIP Do not accept an offer immediately. Request some thinking time.

Nicolas received an on-the-spot offer and was thrilled. This was the job he wanted, and he was anxious to get started. He was going to get an increase in salary from his last job as well as a starting bonus. What more could he ask?

When he got home that evening, he sat down with pencil and paper and began to evaluate the offer and what he was getting overall. He was shocked by his discovery and wished he could go back and talk about some of the issues; unfortunately, he had signed on the dotted line that afternoon.

Nicolas realized the following:

He was offered $55,000 per year plus a hiring bonus of $5,000 paid out quarterly over the next six months. Gain: $10,000.

When he looked over the benefits package, he discovered he now has to pay the insurance premiums for his dependents. His last employer had paid the entire family's premiums. Loss $4,200.

©PhotoDisc, Inc.

His new vacation package provides only two weeks of time off accrued over the next 12 months. His former package included three weeks of vacation. Loss: $962.

In his last position, Nicholas received a 6.6 percent yearly bonus based on company earnings. His new company does not include a planned bonus as part of the salary. Bonuses are earned based on performance and given as deemed appropriate. Loss: $3,250.

His former employer matched 50 cents for every dollar contributed up to 6 percent on his 401K. The new company does not match funds. Loss: $1,500.

Nicolas's calculations showed a loss of $10,000 in the first year of his new job. Nicolas learned the hard way that it is best to take some time to reflect on the total package. Benefits can be worth another 29 to 50 percent of your salary.[1]

Most job offers are made in person or by phone. The person making the offer usually reiterates the job responsibilities and may ask what your salary expectations are. You should have done your homework so you know what you want. Your best strategy is to force him or her to make a monetary offer. Explain that with your skills and the company's need, you are sure the offer will be fair and reasonable. You want to know what he or she is thinking of offering and request information on the company's benefit plan. If your range is below what the employer is planning to pay, he or she will meet your request and save some money. If your range is above what he or she is planning to offer, you may eliminate yourself as a job candidate. Let the company make the offer. Then request more information.

You have received an offer for the job. Display enthusiasm, interest, and pleasure at being selected for the position; however, do not accept immediately. Request some time to consider the offer. Most companies like to have an answer within a day or two. Unless there is an urgency on the part of the company to fill the position immediately, request a minimum of a week. You have some hard thinking to do; you may have additional research to do as well. The more information you can accumulate, the better decision you will be able to make and the better planning you can do for negotiating the deal.

Take this opportunity to ask some questions.

- Determine the start date.
- Request a copy of the position description. Clarify any job responsibilities about which you are vague or unsure.
- Pin down the salary offer.
- Request as much information as possible about the benefit plan— pamphlets, brochures, and so on.

In most cases, negotiating is expected, so you want to be well prepared. Negotiation implies compromise. It is important to understand that you probably will not get everything you want, but the company will not get everything it wants either. Companies want to hire you for the lowest salary possible, and you want to be hired for the greatest salary possible. The objective of negotiation and compromise is to reach an agreement that is satisfactory to both parties. The focus should be on creating a win-win situation.

If you are unable to negotiate the salary you want, perhaps you can get some perks or benefits that will compensate for the difference in salary. You might be able to negotiate paid parking, travel expenses, a company car, gas/mileage, or additional vacation time. It is important you know the value of these perks so you can decide if you have been compensated to your satisfaction. Be wary of one-time perks, such as signing bonuses.

Strategies for Making a Decision

You have some time before you must give the company your decision. How do you spend your time?

Research. Do your homework. You may have an idea of what you are worth, but it is probably more than what the employer has in mind. Your research should provide you with more than just salary expectations. You should investigate the cost value of any benefits that have been offered. What is the value of a stable company in a time of uncertainty? Job security for a lower salary may be more important than a higher salary in a risky business.

Use Your Resources. Get information from similar industries. Trade journals may be beneficial. The Internet, library, newspapers, and magazines may be useful. Use your network. If you have questions or concerns, call the person who made the offer. You are the person he or she chose for the position; therefore, he or she should be happy to help you.

To do your research, use all the resources at your disposal. Review the initial company research that you gathered before the interview. Review the interview evaluation form that you completed. Call on your network. Your network has never been more important than now. Ask questions.

Discuss the offer with family, mentors, friends, even a job consultant if you know one. However, ultimately, the decision is yours. You must do what is best for you. If the position meets the top priority needs that you wrote down, you might decide to accept the job. Evaluate the pros and cons of the offer. Make a decision.

Negotiating the Deal

TIP An employer will not tell you the most he or she is willing to pay.

If you are interested in the position but are not satisfied with the salary, benefits, or vacation time/holiday schedule, you will have to negotiate with the company. Some helpful tips for negotiating are the following:

- Do not be the first to bring up the topic of salary and benefits.
- Implement your persuasive skills. You have to convince the employer you are worth the salary you are asking. The employer must believe he or she is getting his or her money's worth.
- Research thoroughly not only the industry salary averages but also the company salary averages.
- Address the negotiations as compromise, and work together to come to a mutually agreeable solution.

- If monetary compensation cannot be agreed upon, perhaps other perks can be. Consider accepting more responsibility, stock options, or performance-based bonuses. If benefits cannot be agreed upon, look at greater monetary compensation.
- Offer more than one option. If you provide possible solutions to a disparity between your needs and wants and the company's willingness to pay, you display your creativity and problem-solving ability. This creates a positive impression in the employer's mind.
- Emphasize to the employer the benefits of accepting your offer. What does the employer win through this negotiation? An employer is more likely to accept your offer if he or she believe there is a benefit in doing so.
- When negotiating a deal, be assertive, not aggressive. Be professional at all times. Defend your request for increased salary or extended benefits by emphasizing your skills and qualifications.

Communicating Your Decision

Whatever you decide, you should communicate your decision to the company as soon as you make up your mind. Communicate your decision in writing, and present it face-to-face if possible. Otherwise inform the company by telephone.

Accepting the Position. Once you have accepted an offer with a new company, you must inform your current employer that you will be resigning. You should tell your supervisor in a face-to-face meeting if at all possible. Follow this meeting with a letter of resignation. You should attempt to leave on a positive note. You cannot predict the future, and you may be able to benefit from the goodwill you established with the organization. If the company has a policy for giving notice of resignation, follow the policy; for example, the company may require a two-week or 30-day notice.

A letter of resignation should include the date of notification, the date of your last day of employment, a reason for leaving, and something positive about your experience in working for the company. The letter should be addressed to your supervisor and a courtesy copy sent to the human resources department.

Rejecting the Offer. If you have decided not to accept the offer of a position, you should inform the person who made the offer as soon as feasibly possible. Be honest in your reason for not accepting. If you state salary as a reason but you are really rejecting the offer because of the extensive travel required, he or she may meet your salary request. You would then appear to be dishonest if you had to say it really wasn't the salary at all but the travel that caused you to reject the offer.

Strategies for Preparing for the New Job

In your effort to leave on a positive note, complete or update all work or projects before leaving the company. Leave thorough notes and instructions for the person who will take your position. Leave behind good foundations and bridges. You never know when you may need them.

Overlap time for training your successor is the ideal situation. Being available for one or two weeks would be helpful to both the company and the new person in the job. Be available to answer questions for a week or so after leaving.

Be professional even if you are leaving under less than ideal circumstances. Getting even is never an acceptable workplace behavior.

If you can arrange it, give yourself a week or two between jobs to clear your head of one and prepare for the other. Leaving an old job on Friday and starting a new one on Monday allows no time for you to adjust to your new position.

RECAP OF KEY CONCEPTS

- Before receiving an offer, determine your needs and do your homework.
- At the time an offer is made, determine the start date, request a copy of the job description, pin down the salary offer, and request information about the company's benefit program.
- When deciding whether to accept or reject an offer, do your research and use your resources to assist with your decision.
- If negotiating for a better offer, do not be the first to mention the topic of money. Implement your persuasive skills and research thoroughly. Address the negotiations as compromise so you create a win/win situation. Offer more than one option. Emphasize the benefits to the employer. Be assertive, not aggressive; maintain a professional attitude at all times.
- After accepting a new position, you must inform your current employer of your decision to leave by writing a letter of resignation. If you are rejecting an offer, you must inform the person making the offer of your decision as soon as feasibly possible.
- Leave on a positive note, and be available to your successor for a week or so after leaving.

Endnotes

Topic 1 – The Interview: What it Is and Is Not

1. Martin Yate, *Knock 'Em Dead 1999*, Adams Media Corporation, Holbrook, MA, 1999, pp. 87-89.
2. Caryl Rae Krannich and Ronald L. Krannich, *Interviewing for Success*, 7th ed., Impact Publications, Manassas Park, VA, 1998, pp. 18-30.
3. Ibid.

Topic 2 – Frequently Asked Questions

1. Patsy Fulton-Calkins, *Technology & Procedures for Administrative Professionals*, 12th Ed., South-Western Publishing, Cincinnati, OH, 2003, p. 362.

Topic 3 – Interviewing Styles

1. http://www.jobweb.com/resources/Library/, *Tips for Dining with Prospective Employers*, pp. 1-2.
2. Krannich and Krannich, p. 53.
3. Ibid., pp. 53-54.
4. http://www.jobweb.com/resources/Library/Interviews_Resumes, *How to Come Out First in the Second Interview*, pp. 1-2.
5. http://www.accountemps.com/pressroom, *So, What Can You Tell Me About Our Firm?* pp. 1-2.
6. Ibid., p. 2.

Topic 4 – Strategies for Planning, Preparing, and Practicing

1. Joe Griffith, *Speaker's Library of Business Stories, Anecdotes, and Humor*, Prentice Hall, Englewood Cliffs, NJ, 1990, p. 172.
2. Ibid., p. 173.
3. Ibid.
4. Ann Cooper, *The Professional Image*, South-Western Publishing, Cincinnati, OH, 2003.
5. Karyn Repinski, *The Complete Idiot's Guide to Successful Dressing*, Alpha Books, A Division of Macmillan General Reference, New York, 1999, p. 151.
6. Dennis Waitley, *The Psychology of Winning, The Ten Qualities of a Total Winner*, Nightingale-Conant, 1987, Niles, IL, p. 4.

Topic 5 – Strategies for Impressing, Expressing, and Egressing

1. Griffith, p. 172.
2. http://www.editorial.careers.msn.com/gettinghired/interviewing
3. Ibid.
4. Ibid.
5. Griffith, p. 172.
6. Krannich, and Krannich, pp. 106-107.
7. http://www.editorial.careers.msn.com/gettinghired/interviewing

Topic 6 – Strategies for Handling the Tough Questions/Obstacles

1. Equal Employment Opportunity Commission.
2. Michelle Tullier, *The Unofficial Guide to Acing the Interview*, Macmillan General Reference, A Simon and Schuster Macmillan Company, New York, 1999, p. 300.
3. Ibid.
4. Ibid.
5. Ibid.
6. http://www.editorial.careers.msn.com/gettinghired/interviewing
7. Equal Employment Opportunity Commission.

Topic 8 – Strategies for Negotiating the Deal

1. http://www.editorial.careers.msn.com/gettinghired/negotiating

Online Resources

The Interview: What It Is and Is Not
http://www.job-interview.net/
http://www.quintcareers.com/
http://www.collegegrad.com/intv/

Frequently Asked Questions
http://www.quintcareers.com/interview-question-database/
http://www.job-interview.net/interviewgen.htm

Interviewing Styles
http://www.employu.com/jobhunt
http://www.careerbuilder.com
http://www.careers.build.com/career/
http://www.quintcareers.com/job_interviews.html

Strategies for Planning, Preparing, and Practicing
http://www.mapping-your-future.org/planning/thejobin.htm
http://www.quintcareers.com/researching_companies.html

Strategies For Impressing, Expressing, And Egressing
http://www.gisleson.com/articles/interviewindex/
http://www.careerbuilder.com/

Strategies For Handling The Tough Questions/Obstacles
http://www.eeoc.gov/facts
http://www.careercity.com/content/interview/during/illegal.asp
http://www.job-interview.net/interviewgen.htm

Strategies For Assessing, Critiquing, and Evaluating
http://www.adm.uwaterloo.ca/infocecs/CRC/manual/jobworkinterview.html
http://www.thejobpage.com/careerwise/htm

Strategies for Negotiating the Deal
http://www.swz-jobinterview.salary.com/salarywizard/
http://www.acinet.org/acinet/library.htm
http://www.rileyguide.com/offers.html

Post-Assessment Activity

TRUE/FALSE

Directions: Read each of the following statements carefully. Circle T if the statement is true and F if the statement is false.

1. T F A job interview is an opportunity for an employer to examine the qualifications of a job seeker for a position in the company.

2. T F At the beginning of the interview, the interviewer will often converse with you on general topics, such as the weather or local interest issues. Do not be concerned about your responses, as these discussions have nothing to do with the job interview.

3. T F Technology has had minimal impact on interviewing techniques.

4. T F A poor first impression can be overcome.

5. T F Being prepared to handle frequently asked questions is the best way to help you relax and relieve some of the stress and nervousness associated with interviewing.

6. T F During an informal/discussion interview, the interviewer usually asks the same questions of each job applicant for a position.

7. T F The purpose of the meal interview is to observe how an applicant conducts himself or herself in a social situation.

8. T F The most qualified applicant always gets the job.

9. T F A personal mission statement should define who you are, why you exist, and what you will do to become the person you want to be.

10. T F Corporate culture is the environment of unwritten rules of behavior and values that influence the way business is conducted in the workplace.

11. T F Nervousness occurs before and during the interview because of the fear of rejection.

12. T F A calming technique used to control nervousness is concentrating on the outcome of the interview.

13. T F "What foreign languages do you speak?" is a legal question.

14. T F "Are you a Democrat or a Republican?" is a legal question.

15. T F If you are not interested in the position for which you interviewed, you do not need to send a follow-up thank-you letter to the interviewer.

MULTIPLE CHOICE

Directions: Read each of the following statements carefully. Circle the letter of the best response for each statement:

1. Your goal as the job seeker is to
   a. understand what the employer wants and try to match your skills and abilities to those needs.
   b. use the interview as an opportunity to learn more about the position and the organization.
   c. make an effective and professional impression on the interviewer(s).
   d. all of the above.

2. If an interviewer requests that you "Tell me about yourself," your best response would include
   a. a detailed discussion of your work experience.
   b. an overview of the work and education, that have prepared you for the position.
   c. a description of your plans for child care.
   d. personal information that may help the employer make an informed decision.

3. Your reference list should NOT include the names and addresses of the following people:
   a. friends who can attest to your loyalty and dependability
   b. supervisors or instructors who can attest to the quality and quantity of your work
   c. relatives who can attest to your honesty and reliability
   d. coworkers who can attest to your teamwork skills and work ethic

4. Questions about salary expectations should be
   a. answered by requesting information about the company's benefit package.
   b. answered with a specific amount that you learned from your research.
   c. avoided and left up to the generosity of the employer.
   d. deflected and a vague, nonspecific answer given.

5. Which of the following interview types deliberately set up uncomfortable situations for the applicant?
   a. selection
   b. hiring
   c. screening
   d. stress

6. The most common deficiency among job applicants is the lack of
   a. knowledge about the company with whom they are interviewing.
   b. preparation to discuss career plans and goals.
   c. enthusiasm and interest in the company or the position.
   d. experience and preparation for the position.

7. The documentation you need to gather before interviewing includes
   a. your resume.
   b. a list of questions to ask.
   c. your social security card.
   d. all of the above.

8. A self-confident person
    a. does not possess positive self-esteem.
    b. does not have a positive sense of self-worth.
    c. is not self-centered.
    d. all of the above.

9. During your question time, which of the following questions should you NOT ask?
    a. What benefits do you offer?
    b. Why is the position available?
    c. What qualities are you seeking in the candidate for the position?
    d. When are you anticipating making a decision about the position?

10. Which of the following is a good strategy to use to overcome nervousness?
    a. Eat a good breakfast.
    b. Think of the interview as an information-gathering process.
    c. Concentrate on the importance of the interview in meeting your goals.
    d. Focus on the importance of your performance in the outcome of the interview.

11. Which of the following is the best strategy to use when answering an illegal interview question?
    a. Answer the question.
    b. Deflect the question.
    c. Deal with the concern behind the question, and ignore the question itself.
    d. Refuse to answer the question.

12. After the interview, the most important thing to do is
    a. evaluate your performance.
    b. get clothing ready for the next interview.
    c. thank your references.
    d. wait patiently for the employer to call.

13. In your thank-you letter to the interviewer for a position you want, you should
    a. express your appreciation for his or her time and consideration of your skills and abilities.
    b. restate your interest in the position.
    c. explain why you want to work for the company.
    d. all of the above.

14. When the job offer is made, you should
    a. accept the offer if you want the job.
    b. request thinking time.
    c. research salaries in comparable industries.
    d. compare the offer to what your friends are earning.

15. A factor to consider when facing the salary issue includes
    a. geographical location.
    b. your qualifications.
    c. the value of the benefits package offered.
    d. all of the above.

Notes

Notes

Notes

Notes

Notes

Notes

Notes

Notes

Notes

Notes

Notes

Notes

Notes

Notes

Notes

Notes

Notes